PREPARING FOR THE
SHIFT

KATHLEEN DEVINE

Printed in the United States of America

ISBN 979-8-89114-019-6 (sc)
ISBN 979-8-89114-020-2 (hc)
ISBN 979-8-89114-021-9 (e)

Library of Congress Control Number: 2023919391

2023.10.13

MainSpring Books
5901 W. Century Blvd
Suite 750
Los Angeles, CA, US, 90045

www.mainspringbooks.com

Dedication

This book is dedicated to:

My Soul
who has worked with the Creator
for 35,000 years
to prepare
for the upcoming shift

My Husband
who supported me
for 40 years
in my struggle to evolve

My Son
who makes me laugh
and reminds me that
the role I play on Earth
is not my real life

and My Daughter
who reminds me that
I do not have to be perfect

CONTENTS

INTRODUCTION

Namaste everyone. This book is dedicated to the shift and how to prepare for the shift. The first question that needs to be answered is "What is the shift?".

Scientists define the shift as when Earth's rotation slows down, stops and restarts in the opposite direction. Do not be alarmed. Scientists who study the patterns on the ocean floor report that a shift occurs every 26,000 years. This decrease in Earth's rotational speed and change in Earth's rotational direction is a natural phenomenon. Wave patterns on the ocean floor confirm that every 26,000 years, Earth's rotational speed slows down, stops for an estimated three days and then Earth starts rotating in the opposite direction.

Earth is preparing for another shift. Scientists who study the ocean floor report that Earth's rotational speed began to decrease 2,000 years ago. In 1997, Gregg Braden, author of Awakening to Zero Point, reported that scientists recorded a 38% decrease in Earth's rotational speed within the last 2,000 years. As of 2020, Earth's rotational speed has decreased 50%.

A shift is coming. It is just a matter of when.

If you choose to read this book, you will learn about three Earth changes involved with the next shift: decreased Earth's rotational speed, decreased Earth's magnetic force and increased Earth's pulse. You will learn how these three Earth changes are affecting climate change. In addition, you will learn that although Earth is ready for the shift, human beings are not ready.

Human beings have influence over the upcoming shift. If you continue to read this book, you will learn how to prepare for the upcoming shift. The fact is, you have already started to prepare. Just by reading this introduction you have been introduced to the natural phenomenon related to Earth's shifts. When the shift comes, you can use this book as a reference.

If you decide to read this book, you will learn how the three Earth changes are influencing biological forms. In addition, you will learn why human beings do not automatically adapt to Earth's changes and how to recognize when the shift begins.

Preparation for the upcoming shift is up to you. You can wait until the shift begins and use this book as a reference OR you can prepare your energy system to adapt to Earth's changes. The choice is yours.

PROLOGUE

Truth Versus Belief

This prologue is dedicated to the difference between truth and belief. I will provide a general overview. Those of you who would like more detail are encouraged to read Gregg Braden's book <u>The Spontaneous Healing of Belief</u>.

Truth is a function of the cranial brain. At birth, the infant's truth is that she cannot take care of her physical needs. The infant's cranial brain develops filters based on her caregiver's response to her crying. Children develop their initial truth based on their observations and experiences with their caregivers. A child's truth is initially a mirror of her caregiver's truth.

Truth changes as children begin to interact with people who are not their primary caregivers. New observations and experiences with teachers and peers will develop new cranial filters and a child's truth will change. What a child thinks is true at the age of eight may be different at the age of sixteen. Similarly, new adult experiences may change a childhood truth.

For example, my initial truth was that boys were important and girls were not important. Before the age of two, my truth was that I was safer if I did not complain, remained quiet and became invisible. By the age of seven, my truth was that I was stupid. These truths were based on the way I was treated by my parents.

When I was twelve years old, my grandmother moved into my home. She provided new experiences and my truth changed. Girls became as important as boys. I did not need to be invisible to be safe. I was not stupid.

Since no two people on Earth have the exact same experience, no two people have the exact same truth. People who have similar experiences may have similar truths, but everyone's truth is unique.

What is true for me may not be true for you.

When an emotional feeling is added to our truth, our truth becomes our belief. Beliefs are also individual. What I believe may be different from what you believe.

Truth combined with fear or anger creates a different belief than truth combined with love or hope. For example, for many years the truth for human beings was that the earth was flat. Sailors who fueled this truth with fear created the belief that if they sailed too far away from land, their ship would fall off the earth, like falling down a waterfall.

Fortunately, there were sailors who fueled this truth with hope. The hopeful sailors created the belief that the earth would not end and they could keep sailing until they sighted new land.

Like your initial truth, your initial beliefs were based on your observations and experiences with your caregivers as children, combined with the emotional undertone of these experiences. When children learn their lessons from loving, patient, compassionate adults, they initially believe that they are valuable and important. In contrast, when children learn their lessons from fearful, angry and controlling adults, they initially believe that they are not important, not perfect enough and not good enough.

Your beliefs change with new experiences just like your truth changes with new experiences. Your beliefs as a child may be different from your beliefs as an adolescent as you experience new people. Similarly, new adult experiences may create new beliefs.

Preparing for the Shift presents my truth and my beliefs about the upcoming shift. I invite you to read about the three Earth changes that are moving Earth toward the next shift. If these three Earth changes become a part of your truth, I encourage you to fuel this truth with hope.

EARTH CHANGES

E arth is presently experiencing three major changes: decreased Earth's rotational speed, decreased Earth's magnetic force and increased Earth's electrical pulse. I will provide a general overview. Those of you who would like more detail are encouraged to read Gregg Braden's book Awakening to Zero Point.

Earth's Rotational Change

Scientists who study the patterns on the ocean floor report that Earth's rotational speed began to decrease 2000 years ago. In 1997, Gregg Braden, author of Awakening to Zero Point, reported that scientists recorded a 38% decrease in Earth's rotational speed within the last 2000 years. As of 2020, Earth's rotational speed has decreased 50%.

Earth's rotational speed has decreased before. By studying the ocean floor with advanced technology, scientists report that Earth's rotational speed decreases and stops every 26,000 years. Scientists estimate that the stop in Earth's rotation lasts approximately three days. When Earth's rotation starts up again, Earth rotates in the opposite direction. This stopping of Earth's rotation and the change in rotational direction is known as a shift.

Please try a visualization. Raise the index finger of your right hand. Imagine that the finger represents the outer crust of Earth. Rotate the imaginary Earth (index finger) in a circular direction, slow the speed of the imaginary Earth, stop the circular rotation for three seconds and reverse the circular motion of the imaginary Earth. You have just demonstrated a shift with your index finger.

During these Earth shifts, Earth experienced earthquakes, loss of continents and drastic changes in the weather. Fifty-two thousand years ago, the sun rose in the east and set in the west. During a shift, the continent of Lemuria sank into the ocean. Lemuria was the land mass between Asia and the western coast of North America. After the shift, the sun rose in the west and set in the east. Twenty-six thousand years ago another shift occurred. During this shift, the city of Atlantis sank into the ocean. After the shift, the sun rose in the east and set in the west.

Do not be alarmed. This decrease in Earth's rotational speed is a natural phenomenon that occurs every 26,000 years. As Earth's rotational speed decreases, the length of our day becomes longer. Earth's day is now longer than 24 hours. The National Bureau of Standards in Bolder, Co periodically resets the atomic clock to adjust for the longer day so that you will not be frightened.

Preparing for the Shift is dedicated to telling you the truth about Earth's rotational speed. I believe that you will fuel this truth with faith and hope.

Earth's Magnetic Force Change

The decrease in Earth's rotational speed is decreasing Earth's magnetic force. Magnetic force is created when electricity flows in a circular pattern around a fixed body of iron.

Please try a visualization. Create an imaginary iron bar with your left index finger by making a fist and sticking your index finger up.

Imagine electricity coming out of your right index finger and circle the imaginary electricity around your imaginary iron bar. When the speed of your imaginary electricity becomes fast enough, your imaginary iron bar will create a magnetic force field. Move your right index finger to the top of your imaginary iron bar. Now move the right index finger away from the top of the imaginary iron bar and make a circle down to the knuckle of your left index finger. Return the right index finger to the top of the imaginary iron bar and make a circle on the opposite side of the imaginary iron bar down to the knuckle of your left index finger. You have drawn the magnetic force created by the imaginary electricity rotating around your imaginary iron bar.

Scientists define magnetic force as flowing from north to south. Therefore, the tip of your left index finger represents north and the knuckle of your left index finger represents south.

The size of your magnetic force is dependent on the speed of the electrical force circulating around the stationary iron. Please return to your visualization. Increase the speed of the imaginary electricity (right index finger) and then move the right index finger to the top of the imaginary iron bar. Draw a larger circle down to the knuckle of the left index finger and repeat on the opposite side. Your imaginary magnetic force increased in size when you increased the speed of your imaginary electricity.

The direction of your magnetic force is dependent on the direction of your imaginary electricity. Please return to your visualization. Reverse the circular motion of your imaginary electricity. Move your right index finger to the knuckle of the left index finger and draw a circle up to the top of your imaginary iron bar. Your imaginary magnetic force has changed direction. Since scientists consistently define magnetic flow as flowing from north to south, the knuckle of your left index finger now represents north and the tip of your left index finger now represents south.

I want to take your understanding of magnetic force and apply this understanding to Earth. Earth is made up of four major layers. The inner core is made of solid iron and nickel. Although the inner core rotates, the rotational speed of the inner core is so much slower than the outer layers that the inner core represents an "almost fixed" body of iron. The outer core is a molten layer that rotates around the inner core in a circular motion. The mantle makes up most of Earth's mass, is mostly solid rock and rotates in the same circular direction as the outer core. The crust layer is what we see as continents and oceans. The crust rotates in the same circular direction as the outer core and the mantle.

The rotation of the crust, mantle and outer core around the inner core creates a circular electrical charge. Please return to your visualization. Your left finger becomes the inner core of Earth. Your right finger becomes the electrical charge created by the crust, mantle and outer core rotating around the inner core. Your drawing of a magnetic force from the tip of your left finger to the knuckle of your left finger becomes the magnetic force for Earth. The tip of your left finger becomes the north pole and the knuckle of your left finger becomes the south pole.

Just to recap, Earth's rotational speed has been decreasing for the last 2,000 years. As the rotational speed of the three outer Earth layers decreases around the inner core of Earth, the rotational speed of the electrical charge created by the outer layers of Earth decreases. The decrease in rotational speed of the electrical charge created by the outer layers of Earth decreases Earth's magnetic force.

As Earth's magnetic force is decreasing, Earth's magnetic fields are shifting. With the development of satellite technology, scientists can measure Earth's magnetic force and create maps of Earth's magnetic fields around the world. If you are interested, you can find these maps on the internet. I found it interesting that the strength of Earth's magnetic force varies throughout the world. Earth's magnetic force is stronger at the poles and weaker at the equator. If you look at the United States, Earth's magnetic force is stronger over the southern states and weaker over the northern and western states. Similarly, Earth's magnetic force is stronger over the Middle East and weaker over Europe. Mapping of Earth's magnetic fields allows scientists to measure a gradual shift in the north and south poles.

Earth's Electrical Pulse Change

Earth has a "heart beat", an electrical pulse that travels from the outer Earth layers to the ionosphere. The ionosphere is an electrically charged section of the fourth atmospheric layer above Earth.

The first scientist to measure a pulse propagated through Earth was Nikola Telsa, a researcher in Colorado Springs. Telsa made his discovery around 1900. The same Earth pulse was measured by a German scientist, W.O. Schumann, in 1952. From 1952 through 1957, Schumann measured the frequency of Earth's electrical pulse in the ionosphere.

Earth's electrical pulse is increasing. Scientists studying Earth's electrical pulse concur that the frequency of Earth's pulse has been 7.8 Hz for over 200,000 years. In 1990, scientists began to record an increase in the frequency of Earth's electrical pulse and in 1994 the frequency of Earth's electrical pulse was recorded as 8.6 Hz. In 2004, Earth's electrical pulse frequency was 10.5 Hz and in 2020, Earth's electrical pulse frequency was 12.7 Hz.

Scientists believe that the increase in Earth's electrical pulse frequency is a response to the decrease in Earth's magnetic force. They propose that the ionosphere's ability to hold Earth's electrical pulse is declining as Earth's magnetic force decreases. To compensate for the decline in the ionosphere's ability to hold Earth's electrical pulse, Earth's frequency of transmission is increasing.

As Earth's electrical pulse is increasing toward 13 Hz, scientists predict that a significant biological change is coming. Scientists have a special series of numbers known as the Fibonacci mathematical series for predicting biological events. The Fibonacci series is: 1+1=2, 1+2=3, 2+3=5, 3+5=8. The number 8 is close to 7.8 Hz which was the frequency of Earth's electrical pulse for the last 200,000 years. The next number in the Fibonacci sequence is 5+8=13. Scientists predict that when the frequency of Earth's electrical pulse reaches 13 Hz a major biological change will occur.

Earth appears to have a domino effect going on. Earth's rotational speed is slowing down which is causing Earth's magnetic force to decrease. The decrease in Earth's magnetic force is making it difficult for the ionosphere to sustain Earth's electrical pulse and to compensate, the frequency of Earth's electrical pulse is increasing.

These three Earth changes are creating an increase in seismic activity (more earthquakes and new fault lines), changes in weather patterns (more hurricanes, more flooding in some areas and more drought in other areas) and an overall increase in Earth's temperature.

If Earth stops rotating, Earth's magnetic force ceases and Earth's electrical pulse increases to 13 Hz all at the same time, a major biological change will occur during the next shift. The next shift will not be the same as the shifts in the past.

EARTH CHANGES AFFECT BIOLOGICAL FORMS

N ow that you know that the frequency of Earth's electrical pulse is increasing, I want to explain how this increase in frequency is affecting biological forms. But first, I want to explore the truth about atoms.

Before 1920, scientists believed the atom looked like our solar system. Electrons and protons rotate around the nucleus like the planets rotate around the sun. The space between the electrons, protons and nucleus was empty. This is what I was taught in high school and in college. My truth about the atom was that the space between electrons, protons and nucleus was empty.

My truth about the atom changed when I learned about the energy inside the atom. Advanced technology allowed scientists to discover this energy inside of the atom. The first electron microscope was developed in 1932. After 1932, scientists developed technology that allowed them to see the "empty space" that is called air. Scientists removed all of the air from a tube creating a "vacuum" of empty space. With the use of technology, scientists could see that the "empty space" was filled with energy particles never seen before.

Scientists called these energy particles quantum particles.

As technology advanced, scientists were able to see that the "empty space" within an atom was filled with concentric electrical energy rings. After learning about the electrical energy that filled the atom, my truth about the atom changed. All atoms are made up of energy with electrons, protons and nucleus positioned inside the concentric electrical energy rings.

Now, I want to present how atoms create all physical life forms. Atoms combine to form cells. Scientists are able to measure a small voltage coming from a single cell indicating that the composite energy from the atoms creates a signature energy frequency for each cell.

Biological cells combine to form tissues such as plant or animal tissues. Animal tissues include organs, bone, muscle, nerve and skin. With technology, scientists are able to record a signature energy frequency for each tissue (organ, muscle, bone, etc.) indicating that the composite energy from the cells creates a signature energy frequency for each tissue. When an organ, muscle or bone is diseased, the signature frequency of the organ, muscle or bone decreases. This lower energy frequency reflects the disease. In contrast, healthier cells create a higher energy frequency in the tissue.

All life forms have a base energy frequency. This base energy frequency is a composite of all of the major energy frequencies within the biological form. If all tissues are healthy in a plant or animal, the base energy frequency will be higher. One diseased organ may not influence the base energy frequency of the life form. However, multiple organ disease or multiple tissues with a decreased energy frequency, will decrease the base energy frequency of the life form.

In addition to being influenced by the health of a life form's tissue, the base frequency of all life forms is influenced by the frequency of Earth's electrical pulse. All life forms are electrical entities living on Earth, another electrical entity. When two electrical entities with different frequencies are placed near each other, the entity with the lower electrical frequency will try to match the entity with the higher electrical frequency. This phenomenon is known as electronic resonance.

All plants and animals on Earth automatically resonate with Earth's electrical pulse. For the last 200,000 years, the frequency of Earth's electrical pulse was 7.8 Hz. Therefore, the average base frequency for all plants and animals was 7.8 Hz. When the frequency of Earth's electrical pulse began to increase, the cells within all plants and animals began to seek electronic resonance with Earth's electrical pulse. This means that the base frequency of all plants and animals is increasing and keeping up with the frequency of Earth's electrical pulse.

Although human beings are also electrical entities, human beings do not automatically resonate with Earth's electrical pulse because the base frequency of human beings is influenced by their emotional state. Scientists are able to measure the frequency of emotional energies within the heart. Lower frequency emotional energies include fear, hate, jealousy, despair, depression, shame and sadness. Higher frequency emotional energies include love, compassion, peace, joy, gratitude and appreciation. Human beings have the ability to hold on to lower frequency or higher frequency emotional energies. If a human being consistently holds on to lower frequency emotional energies, the cellular electrical energy will maintain a lower energy frequency and the human being's base frequency will not be able to increase to resonate with Earth's electrical pulse. In contrast, if a human being consistently holds on to higher frequency emotional energies, the cellular electrical energy will maintain a higher energy frequency and the human being's base frequency will be able to increase to resonate with Earth's electrical pulse.

The major difference between human beings and other animals is that the Creator gave human beings free will. Human beings are free to choose the truths they will accept. They are free to choose the emotional energy that will fuel their truths to form their beliefs.

Although it is true that a child's truths and beliefs are first introduced to them by their caregivers, an adolescent will begin to rebel and form new truths and beliefs. Human beings are free to change their beliefs or change the emotional fuel for their beliefs. They are free to choose between lower frequency emotional energies associated with fear and higher frequency emotional energies associated with love.

The majority of human beings are choosing to maintain their lower frequency fear beliefs. These beliefs keep the cellular energy frequency low and prevent them from resonating with Earth's electrical pulse. This inability to resonate with Earth's electrical pulse is manifesting in two major areas: increased disease and increased conflict.

Having a base frequency that is below Earth's electrical pulse is like walking around in a mud pit. The lower base frequency makes everything more difficult. Human beings experience this mud pit as conflict and disease.

When the base frequency of an individual is below the frequency of Earth's electrical pulse, the signature frequency of the individual's organs and nervous system is below Earth's electrical pulse. When biological cells are unable to keep up with Earth's electrical pulse, the cells become diseased. This is why physicians are seeing an increase in cancer, strokes, heart disease, Alzheimer's disease, dementia, Parkinson's disease and multiple sclerosis. These diseases are directly related to the lower base frequency of the physical body.

As the difference between the individual's base frequency and Earth's electrical pulse increases, the individual's fears related to control intensify. This intensified lower frequency energy is manifested as increased conflict between different people. Human beliefs supported by lower frequency emotional energies intensify dipolar "truths": I am good and you are bad; I am right and you are wrong; white is good and black is bad; black is good and white is bad; Christian is good and Muslim is bad; Muslim is good and Christian is bad. Although these dipolar "truths" have nothing to do with fact, the results of these beliefs are more violence, more hate, more anger, more war and more division between people.

In contrast, many human beings are choosing a different path. These individuals are choosing beliefs fueled with higher frequency emotional energies associated with love. These higher frequency beliefs allow their base frequency to increase and either resonate with Earth's electrical pulse or increase beyond Earth's electrical pulse.

Humans who have a base frequency equal to or above Earth's electrical pulse are less susceptible to disease. The higher energy frequency of the physical body encourages a higher vibration for the individual organs and cells within the physical body. This higher vibration allows the cells and organs to be healthier.

Individuals who are increasing in base frequency focus on cooperation, compromise, compassion and discussion to resolve conflict. The higher frequency emotional energies allow these individuals to listen to diverse beliefs without judgment. These are the individuals who bring hope to the human race.

Let us recap. Earth is changing. Earth's rotational speed is decreasing. The decrease in Earth's rotational speed is decreasing Earth's magnetic force. Earth's decreased magnetic force is creating an increase in Earth's electrical pulse. If Earth's electrical pulse reaches 13 Hz at the same time Earth stops rotating, a biological change will occur. All plants and animals are resonating with Earth's electrical pulse. Therefore, when Earth has a biological change, all plants, animals and human beings who consistently hold on to higher frequency emotional energies will have a biological change. Human beings who consistently hold on to lower frequency emotional energies will not follow Earth's biological change.

Exactly how Earth changes affect your biological form is up to you. You can choose to hold on to your lower frequency emotional energies associated with fear OR you can choose to focus on your higher frequency emotional energies associated with love. The choice is yours.

ENERGY BEINGS

In the last chapter, you learned that the atoms that make up your biological cells are filled with energy. You also learned that your biological cells emit a small electrical voltage that can be measured. Your biological cells create all of your physical tissues (bone, muscle, organs, skin, nerves, blood vessels) and the electrical energy within the biological cells creates a signature energy frequency for each tissue. In addition, you learned that the composite energy from all of your physical tissues creates a base frequency for your physical form. Your life form is made up of physical components, which you can see, and energy particles which most of you cannot see.

Some of you were born with the ability to see the energy particles outside of life forms. This energy field surrounding life forms is called the aura of the life form. Many of you developed the skill of seeing auras of plants, animals and humans through instruction and practice.

Most of us rely on technology to see the aura. The aura surrounding life forms was first discovered in 1939 by a Russian scientist named Semyen Kirlian. In the 1980's, Guy Coggins developed the aura camera and today you can buy an aura camera on the internet.

The aura camera will take a picture of the size, shape and color of your aura. The color of your aura reflects your emotional state. For those of you who would like to explore the meaning of the different auric colors, I refer you to the internet. You will find beautiful auric colors and a variety of meanings for these colors. To prepare for the upcoming shift, you only need to understand that you have an aura.

Preparing for the shift also involves a basic understanding of the chakra system. Chakra means disk, vortex or wheel. Vortex refers to an energy vortex between the aura of the life form and the physical body. Disk and wheel refer to the spinning or rotating of the chakra vortex.

There are seven major chakra vortexes attached to the human life form.

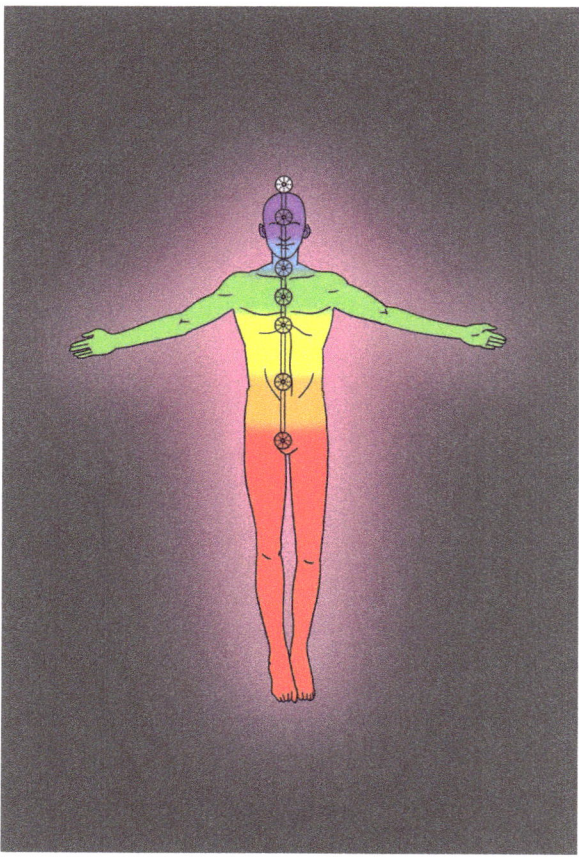

Fig 1

Each chakra spins at a different rate and the spin rate determines the color of the chakra. The first chakra is known as the root chakra, is located at the base of your spine and has a spin rate consistent with the color red. The second chakra is known as the sacral chakra, is located in the pelvic area below your belly button and has a spin rate consistent with the color orange. The third chakra is known as the solar plexus chakra, is located in your navel area and has a spin rate consistent with the color yellow. The fourth charka is known as the heart chakra, is located over your sternum in the center of your chest and has a spin rate consistent with the color green. The fifth chakra is known as the throat chakra, is located in your throat and has a spin rate consistent with the color blue. The sixth chakra is known as the third eye chakra, is located between your eyes and has a spin rate consistent with the color indigo. The seventh chakra is known as the crown chakra, is located at the top of your head and has a spin rate consistent with the color violet.

The seven major chakras function as information energy transformers. All life forms receive information from outside of the life form. Some of this information comes through the life form's physical senses (vision, hearing, taste, smell and touch). Other information comes through the life form's energy body.

The moment a life form comes into contact with an external energy, the life form begins to respond and adjust to the new energy. For example, light energy affects the energy bodies of human beings.

Light energy has a range of frequencies which result in different colors. The effect the color has on the human energy body is determined by the color frequency. Certain colors lower blood pressure, different colors communicate action and other colors communicate authority or trust. Many business owners design the work environment with colors that support calm energies or increased productivity. Some people have developed careers centered around teaching others the effects of light energy on the energy bodies of human beings.

Similarly, some business owners design the work environment with sound energy to affect the energy bodies of the people who work, play or eat there. Restaurant owners who want customers to eat quickly will play faster music. In contrast, restaurant owners who want customers to order more food (appetizers, salad, desert) will play softer music to encourage the energy bodies to relax and increase digestion. Business owners that are encouraging mental learning will play classical music. Classical music relaxes the energy being and stimulates memory and learning. In contrast, owners of health clubs that promote physical exercise will play rock music.

When two human beings meet, the energy bodies for both human beings are checking each other out. Some people "feel" safe or familiar. With other people, you might "feel" guarded, frightened or instantly irritated. With each new encounter, your energy body is receiving, processing or sending information.

The information received by the energy body is filtered through the chakra system. The chakras are energy transformers that decrease the frequency of the information energy received by the energy body so that the information can be absorbed by the biological form. Each chakra has a spin rate that correlates with the frequency of information it receives, and this frequency of information correlates with a specific color. Scientists are able to record the spin rate of these chakras and have determined a range of colors for each chakra. Each color represents a range of spin rates that fall within a specific wavelength of radiant information. All chakras are exposed to all wavelengths of information, but not all wavelengths of information can be received by the chakra. The type of information received by the chakra is dependent upon the spin rate of the chakra.

For example, out of the seven main chakras, the first chakra has the slowest spin rate. Scientists have recorded a range of frequencies for this first chakra within the color spectrum of red. The frequency of energy information that correlates with the spin rate for the first chakra is tribal information. Tribal beliefs, expectations, traditions and prejudices are received by the first chakra. The first chakra is also exposed to information about individual relationships and individual safety but the frequency of this information is higher. This higher frequency information does not correlate with the spin rate of the first chakra and is not received by the first chakra. Individual relationships and individual safety information is received by chakras that have higher spin rates.

The amount of information each chakra can process at any one time is dependent on the spin rate of the chakra. If the chakra is unable to process all of the information received, some of the information is temporarily stored in "buffers". The body will assimilate this stored information at a later time. If the "buffers" become so full that the body cannot assimilate all of the information, the excess information is stored in the biological cells connected to the chakra. Each chakra is connected to biological cells within the physical body. For example, the first chakra is connected to the biological cells in both legs, extending from the hips to the feet. This physical area connected to the first chakra is known as the physical energy field. When the first chakra is unable to process all of the information it is receiving and the buffers are full, the overflow energy information is stored in the physical energy field. This overflow energy information is lower frequency fear energy that decreases the frequency of the biological cell and decreases the signature frequency of the tissue in the physical energy field.

You learned in the last chapter that a decrease in biological cell frequency and a decrease in the signature frequency of tissues increases the potential for disease in the tissue. In addition, if enough lower frequency energies are stored in the tissues and multiple tissues have decreased energy, the base frequency of the life form will decrease. Human beings with a lower base frequency will not be able to resonate with Earth's electrical pulse. You also learned that human beings who choose and hold on to their lower frequency emotional energies will not be able to resonate with Earth's electrical pulse. So how do you choose and hold on to your higher frequency emotional energies?

The answer is that you learn to manage your heart brain. Most people do not even know they have a heart brain. I will provide you with a general overview of the heart brain. For those of you who want a more detailed explanation, I recommend Gregg Braden's book <u>Resilience from the Heart</u>.

All of the emotional energy received from outside human life forms is first received by the heart chakra. The biological cells connected to the heart chakra is called the psyche energy field. The heart brain is located inside the psyche energy field.

The heart brain was discovered in 1991 by Dr. Andrew Armour at the University of Montreal. He found specialized cells that make up the brain and spinal cord located inside of the heart. These specialized cells are made up of neurons, specialized cells that communicate information with other cells using electrical energy and neurites, tiny projections that carry information toward and away from the neuron.

Scientists refer to the heart neurons as the "little brain" in the heart. Since 1991, scientists have discovered that the brain in the heart has a relationship with the brain in the cranium. When studying the heart brain, scientists placed electroencephalogram (EEG) electrodes on a subject's head to record cranial brain waves. Subjects in these experiments were either asked to meditate to a higher emotional state such as love, peace or compassion or asked to watch videos designed to invoke various emotional states ranging from joy and laughter to fear, anger or sadness.

The type of EEG pattern recorded during these experiments depended on the emotional response of the subject. When subjects experienced lower frequency emotional energies such as fear, hate or anger, the EEG recorded chaotic cranial brain wave activity. This chaotic brain wave activity stimulated the cranial brain to send a signal to increase stress hormones. When subjects experienced higher frequency emotional energies (love, compassion, peace, gratitude or appreciation), the EEG recorded harmonized cranial brain wave activity. This harmonized brain wave form stimulated the cranial brain to send a signal to the adrenal glands to decrease stress hormones.

The relationship between the heart brain and the cranial brain is not exclusive to emotional energies and is not one sided. Scientists have discovered that the heart brain is the first brain to recognize physiological changes within the physical body. Physiological changes such as stress, high blood sugar or infection are transferred from the blood chemistry to the heart brain. The heart brain converts the language of blood chemistry to the electrical language of the nervous system. The electrical signal is sent to the cranial brain. The cranial brain responds and sends the needed signal to adjust the blood chemistry. If the body is under stress, a signal is sent to the adrenal glands to produce cortisol and adrenaline. If the body's blood sugar is too high, a signal is sent to the pancreas to produce more insulin. If the body has an infection, a signal is sent to the immune system to produce antibodies.

Communication between the heart brain and the cranial brain goes back and forth. Human beings have known for a long time that they can increase the frequency of their emotional energies with visualization and meditation. You can visualize something that makes you feel happy or makes you smile. The cranial EEG will change to a harmonized wave form and this harmonized wave form will be communicated to your heart brain. Your heart brain will increase the frequency of the emotional energies in your heart chakra and you will feel joy, happy, love or at peace. Similarly, human beings have used meditation to change the cranial EEG to a harmonized wave form for 5000 years. During meditation, the cranial brain will send messages to the physical body to decrease stress and send a harmonized wave form to the heart brain.

Let us recap. Your physical body is surrounded by an energy field known as the aura. Your biological cells are filled with energy and emit a small frequency. You have seven main vortexes that connect your aura with your biological cells known as chakras. Your chakras act as transformers, decrease the frequency of the energy received from outside of your physical body and send this energy to your biological cells. You are an energy being.

The Creator has given you free will. You can choose between maintaining lower frequency emotional energies or maintaining higher frequency emotional energies. You have a heart brain that will help you maintain higher frequency emotional energies. If you choose to resonant with Earth's electrical pulse, you can learn to manage your heart brain. The choice is yours.

EARTH'S EVOLUTION

In the first part of this book, you learned about three Earth changes that are occurring right now. You also learned that one of these changes (increasing frequency of Earth's electrical pulse) will cause a biological change when Earth's electrical pulse reaches 13 Hz. In addition, you learned that all plants and animals are resonating with Earth's electrical pulse which means that all plants and animals will follow Earth's biological change. Since your Creator gave you free will, you can choose to resonate with Earth's electrical pulse or you can choose to stay at a lower base frequency. That decision will determine whether or not you will participate with Earth's biological change during the upcoming shift.

Earth's biological change during the upcoming shift will involve a change in physical form. Since Earth was created, Earth has been holding an electrical pulse frequency of 7.8 Hz which supports third dimensional form. All plants, animals and human beings resonate with Earth's electrical pulse and are presently in third dimensional form. You are able to see and hear all life forms on Earth because they are all in third dimensional form. When Earth's electrical pulse reaches 13 Hz, all life forms that have a base frequency of 13 Hz or higher will change physical form. This new physical form will be called fourth dimensional form.

Changing physical form is not unfamiliar to humans. Many physical forms change from solid to liquid to gas when there is a change in temperature and pressure. Water is the easiest example. When heat is applied to solid water (ice), water molecules increase in energy frequency and become liquid water. When heat is applied to liquid water, the water molecules increase in energy frequency and become steam. The speed at which these changes occur depends on the atmospheric pressure. The higher the atmospheric pressure, the faster the change from solid to liquid to gas. The lower the atmospheric pressure, the slower these changes occur. That is why baking that involves changing a liquid consistency to a solid consistency takes longer at higher altitudes (less atmospheric pressure). Ice and liquid water are within the frequency range that is visible to the human eye. Steam is above the frequency range that is visible to the human eye.

The change from third to fourth dimensional form also involves two variables, the frequency of Earth's electrical pulse and Earth's magnetic force. When Earth's electrical pulse increases to 13 Hz and Earth's magnetic force decreases to almost nothing, part of Earth will evolve to fourth dimensional form. Fourth dimensional form will have a base frequency range that will not be visible to someone who stays in third dimensional form.

In the first part of this book, you learned that Earth's magnetic force is not the same everywhere. Some areas on Earth have a lower magnetic force than others. The parts of Earth that have the lowest magnetic force will begin to evolve to fourth dimensional form first.

I will use the United States as an example. The lowest magnetic force over the United States will be in the northwest and in the northeast. These Earth areas will evolve to fourth dimensional form during the upcoming shift. The southeast and part of the west will have a higher magnetic force. These Earth areas will stay in third dimensional form during the upcoming shift (Fig 2).

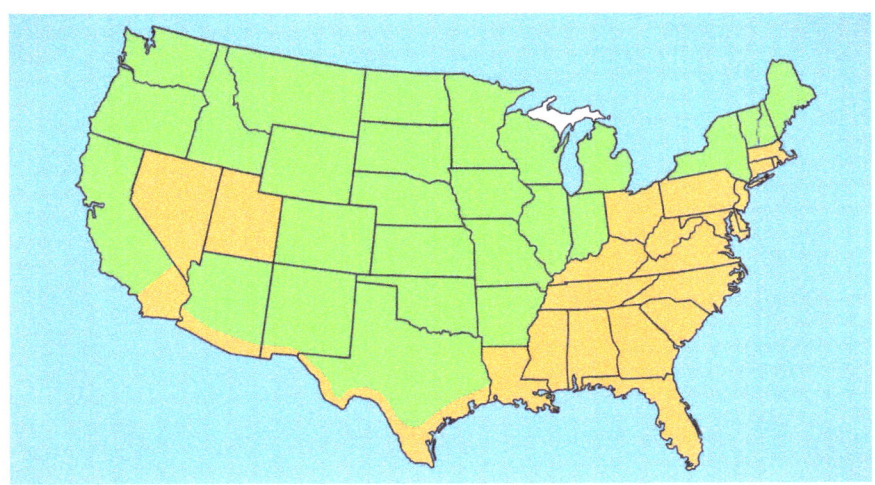

Fig 2
Green = 4th dimensional areas
Orange = 3rd dimensional areas

Not all Earth areas will initially evolve to fourth dimensional form. Earth areas with a low enough magnetic force to evolve to fourth dimensional form will include western Canada, northern Greenland, all of the United Kingdom, all of Norway, western Europe (western part of Spain, France, Germany and Sweden), all of Alaska, northwest Russia, eastern Australia and northern Japan.

You learned in a previous chapter that all plants and animals are resonating with the increased frequency of Earth's electrical pulse. Therefore, all plants and animals in the new fourth dimensional areas will evolve to fourth dimensional form. In contrast, plants and animals living in third dimensional areas will stay in third dimensional form.

Remember that your Creator gave you free will. You can choose to evolve to fourth dimensional form or you can stay in third dimensional form. No matter where you live, if your base frequency is below 13 Hz, you will stay in third dimensional form. If you have a base frequency that resonates with Earth's electrical pulse (13 Hz or higher), you will evolve to fourth dimensional form.

Let us pretend that you and I are standing in the same room at the time of the upcoming shift. You evolve to fourth dimensional form, and I remain in third dimensional form. You would "disappear". My third dimensional eyes would not be able to see you. Your cellular frequency would be vibrating outside of my visual field.

Whether or not you can continue to live where you live now after the upcoming shift will depend on your base frequency and the level of magnetic force in the area where you live. Fourth dimensional form (base frequency of 13 Hz or higher) will be compatible with a lower magnetic force. Similarly, third dimensional form (base frequency below 13 Hz) will be compatible with a higher magnetic force. If your base frequency is not compatible with the magnetic force of your area, you will not survive in that area for very long. You will need to migrate to an area that is compatible with your base frequency.

What does that mean? If you are living in an area that evolves to fourth dimensional form and you evolve to fourth dimensional form, you can stay where you are living. Similarly, if you are living in an area that stays in third dimensional form and you stay in third dimensional form, you can stay where you are living. In contrast, if you are living in an area that evolves to fourth dimensional form and you stay in third dimensional form, you will need to migrate to a third dimensional area. If you are living in a third dimensional area and you evolve to fourth dimensional form, you will need to migrate to a fourth dimensional area.

Before I explain the events of the upcoming shift, I want to explain why the upcoming shift is delayed. The Mayan calendar predicted that the upcoming shift would begin in 2012. Earth was not ready in 2012. Earth's rotation was not slow enough, Earth's magnetic force was not low enough and Earth's electrical pulse was not high enough.

In my first book, Clearing Your Karma Before the Shift, I predicted that the upcoming shift would begin in 2020. Earth was ready in 2020 but human beings were not ready.

Unlike the previous shifts, the upcoming shift is driven by human evolution. Human beings are very special. The human life form is designed to evolve. This evolution involves the energy body of the human life form and the soul of the human life form.

All human beings have a soul. The primary goal for all souls is to become more like the Creator. The Creator holds all energy frequencies but Her primary energy frequencies are higher. She is primarily loving, compassionate and nonjudgmental. She has given all souls free will and the ability to create their own learning experiences. In addition, the Creator created Earth as a learning planet with human beings as embodiments for learning. I call this learning planet Earth school.

When a soul wants to learn, a slice of the soul is sent to Earth school and attached to an embodiment. Since the Creator has given both the soul and the embodiment free will, the embodiment is free to make choices that will allow the soul and the embodiment to learn. When the embodiment dies, the slice of the soul detaches from the embodiment and returns to the soul.

The Creator does not judge or punish the soul or the embodiment for choices made in Earth school. However, there are consequences for the choices made by the human embodiment.

For the last thirty-five thousand years, Earth's electrical pulse of 7.8 Hz has supported lower frequency emotional energies associated with the second chakra. In the previous chapter, you learned that chakras are energy transformers that decrease the frequency of information received by the energy body. In addition, you learned that each chakra has a specific spin rate which correlates with the frequency of specific information. The second chakra's spin rate correlates with relationship information. Specifically, the second chakra receives relationship information related to the physical world and the need to control the physical world.

Your soul has been coming down to Earth school to learn lessons about relationships. These relationships could be with another individual (one on one relationships) or you could be learning about your relationship within a group. In addition, you were learning about your relationship with yourself (personal power within the physical world or your ability to survive in the physical world). The second chakra also receives information about your relationships with food, drugs, money and sex.

Your soul's lessons about relationships have focused on control. What does it feel like to control another individual or what does it feel like to be controlled by another individual. What does it feel like to be controlled by food, alcohol, drugs, money or sex (we call these control relationships addictions).

Control involves working with lower frequency emotional energies. These lower frequency emotional energies include fear, anger, hatred, jealousy, revenge, depression and despair. In addition, sometimes your embodiment's attempt to control others creates physical violence. For the last thirty-five thousand years, you have been learning lessons about war, physical abuse, slavery and sexual abuse.

The Creator is ready for human beings to evolve. She wants all souls that come down to Earth school to complete the two major lessons from the second chakra. These two major lessons are:

1. You have no control over your relationships.
2. Relationships have no control over you.

Once your soul has learned the two basic lessons from the second chakra, your soul will come down to Earth school to learn lessons related to higher frequency emotional energies. The higher frequency emotional energies include love, compassion, appreciation, gratitude, hope, joy and peace. The fourth chakra has the spin rate that correlates with these higher frequency emotional energies.

The evolution of human beings will involve a change in focus from lower frequency emotional energies to higher frequency emotional energies. Earlier in this chapter you also learned that the evolution of human beings will involve a change in physical form. These two changes will occur during the upcoming shift which is why I refer to the upcoming shift as the evolutionary shift.

During the evolutionary shift, human beings who are focused on lower frequency emotional energies related to control will stay in third dimensional form. Human beings who choose to focus on higher frequency emotional energies will evolve to fourth dimensional form.

There will be two primary differences between third dimensional and fourth dimensional human beings. Third dimensional human beings will continue with physical violence and control will continue to be the focus with relationships. In contrast, fourth dimensional human beings will no longer consider physical violence an option. That does not mean that the human beings in fourth dimensional form will not defend themselves. No tolerance for physical violence means that there will be no physical wars, no physical abuse and no sexual abuse. In addition, in the fourth dimensional areas, human beings will focus on relationships with cooperation and compromise rather than control.

Many of you have already learned the two major lessons from the second chakra. You know that you have no control over others and you have no control over events. In addition, you know that others and events do not control you. Control is an illusion. Your focus with relationships is on higher frequency emotional energies that include love, compassion, gratitude and appreciation. When you work with others your focus is on cooperation and compromise.

Do you feel like you are in the minority? If you do, you are correct. You are among the minority.

Please focus on hope. It only takes a minority of human beings to create an evolutionary shift. I will explain why a minority of human beings can make such a significant change by explaining the concept of critical mass.

Critical mass is the specific number of human beings needed to make a group change. It only takes one human being to start the journey toward group change. When one human being demonstrates a new behavior or expresses a new belief, other human beings exposed to the new behavior or new belief will adopt the new behavior or the new belief. When enough human beings within a group demonstrate the new behavior or express the new belief, the whole group of human beings will change. The number at which the whole group changes is the critical mass number.

The change during the evolutionary shift will involve a physical change from third dimensional form to fourth dimensional form. The Creator has set the critical mass number for this physical change at 30%. She wants 30% of the adult human population to evolve into fourth dimensional form during the evolutionary shift. This means that 30% of the adult human population on Earth will be functioning at the higher emotional energy frequency level and will have a base frequency of 13 Hz or higher at the time of the evolutionary shift.

For those of you preparing for the evolutionary shift, the Creator will send you a heads up that the shift is coming. Three months before the evolutionary shift, the embodiments of Mother Mary and Quan Yin will be seen all over Earth. There will be many documented sightings and thousands of people will profess that Mother Mary or Quan Yin appeared and spoke to them. The message brought by Mother Mary and Quan Yin will be one of peace, love and compassion. People preparing for the evolutionary shift will believe these visitations are a sign that the evolutionary shift is coming.

THE EVOLUTIONARY SHIFT

The evolutionary shift will be a three-day event. During the first twenty-four hours, Earth's rotation will slow down to the point that it will appear as if the sun and moon are standing still. People who have prepared for the evolutionary shift will know that the shift is beginning. People who have not prepared for the evolutionary will panic. Many people will believe that the end of the world is coming.

This belief will create an increase in crime.

During the second twenty-four hours, massive earthquakes will destroy major cities all over Earth. New fault lines will form and four major cities will sink into the ocean: Los Angeles, New York City, Washington DC and Rhome, Italy. Millions of people will die.

During the third twenty-four hours, Earth's electrical pulse will increase to just above 13 Hz and part of Earth will evolve from third dimensional form to fourth dimensional form. Fourth dimensional areas will go through a massive cleansing. All materials and products that do not resonate with Earth's higher electrical pulse frequency will vanish.

Petroleum, plastic, toxic waste, fossil fuels, pesticides, plutonium and uranium will no longer be available in fourth dimensional areas. In addition, products that are destructive to the human physical form will vanish. Tobacco products and harmful drugs will no longer be available in fourth dimensional areas. In contrast, third dimensional areas will remain below 13 Hz and these areas will not change.

Materials and products will remain the same.

All plants and animals will resonate with the frequency of the area they are in. Plants and animals in the fourth dimensional areas will resonate with Earth's higher electrical pulse frequency and evolve to fourth dimensional forms. Plants and animals in the third dimensional areas will continue to stay in third dimensional forms.

The evolution of human beings does not depend on where they live. All human beings with a base frequency of 13 Hz or higher will evolve from third dimensional form to fourth dimensional form.

Just to recap. Human beings are driving the evolutionary shift. When 30% of the adult human population reaches a base frequency of 13 Hz or higher, the evolutionary shift will begin. During the three-day evolutionary shift event, part of Earth will evolve to fourth dimensional form, all plants and animals in the fourth dimensional areas will evolve to fourth dimensional form and all human beings with a base frequency of 13 Hz or higher will evolve to fourth dimensional form.

PREPARING FOR THE EVOLUTIONARY SHIFT

I f the evolutionary shift becomes part of your truth, please fuel this truth with hope. There are five ways you can prepare for the evolutionary shift. First you can maintain higher frequency emotional energies by managing your heart brain. Second, you can manage your anxiety by managing your heart brain and using a manual technique to influence your adrenal glands. Third, you can learn how to manage emotional shock. Fourth, you can eliminate the fears stored in your energy fields that create physical violence. Fifth, you can physically prepare.

Managing Your Heart Brain

Before I tell you how to manage your heart brain, I want to tell you how you can use your heart brain to influence others. In a previous chapter, you learned that scientists doing research on the heart brain placed electroencephalogram (EEG) electrodes on subjects' heads to record cranial brain waves. These scientists discovered a correlation between the emotional response of the subject and the cranial brain waves recorded by the EEG. Lower frequency emotional energies (fear, anger, etcetera) correlated with chaotic brain wave activity. In contrast, higher frequency emotional energies (love, compassion, etcetera) correlated with harmonized cranial brain wave activity.

In the 1990s, scientists at the HeartMath Institute discovered a relationship between heart rate variability (HRV) and the frequency of emotional energies. Heart rate variability is the variation of time between heart beats which is controlled by the autonomic nervous system. Scientists placed electrodes over the subject's heart to record the HRV with an electrocardiogram (ECG) and electrodes on the subject's head to record cranial brain waves with the electroencephalogram (EEG). Subjects watched videos designed to invoke various emotional states ranging from joy and laughter to fear, anger or sadness.

The type of HRV waveform recorded during these experiments depended on the frequency of the emotional response of the subject. When subjects experienced lower frequency emotional energies (fear, anger or sadness), the ECG recorded chaotic HRV waveforms. When subjects experienced higher frequency emotional energies (joy or laughter), The ECG recorded harmonized HRV waveforms.

The HRV waveform is sent to the amygdala (the part of the limbic system in the brain where emotions are given meaning and emotional memories are stored) through the autonomic nervous system via the heart brain. The cells inside the amygdala synchronize with the HRV waveform. If the HRV waveform is chaotic, the waveform within the amygdala is chaotic. Similarly, if the HRV waveform is harmonized, the waveform within the amygdala is harmonized. The amygdala interprets chaotic waveforms as lower frequency emotional energies such as fear, anger or anxiety and harmonized waveforms as higher frequency emotional energies such as love, joy, happiness or peace.

The amygdala sends the chaotic or harmonized waveform pattern to the upper brain and the upper brain's EEG will synchronize with the amygdala waveform. If the amygdala waveform is chaotic, the EEG will have a chaotic waveform and the cranial brain will send a signal to the adrenal glands to increase stress hormones. In contrast, if the amygdala waveform is harmonized, the EEG will have a harmonized waveform and the cranial brain will send a signal to the adrenal glands to decrease stress hormones.

In addition to studying the heart's HRV waveform, scientists at the HeartMath Institute established that the heart emits an electromagnetic energy. This electromagnetic energy from the heart extends out beyond the physical body. Once this heart electromagnetic energy was discovered, scientists began studying how this electromagnetic energy might affect other life forms.

Scientists placed ECG electrodes on a human being and a pet dog or horse. The HRV waveforms for the human being and the pet were recorded. The human being was instructed to increase her emotional energies and the HRV waveforms from the human being and the pet were recorded. When the human being's HRV waveforms were harmonized, the pet's HRV waveforms were harmonized. When the human being left the pet's space, the pet's HRV waveform returned to the initial waveform recorded before the human being increased her emotional energies. Scientists hypothesized that harmonized HRV waveforms were emitted from the human being via the electromagnetic force extending from the human being's heart. The pet received the electromagnetic force from the human being and the pet's HRV waveform synchronized with the human being's HRV waveform.

In addition to studying how HRV waveforms from a human being can affect an animal, scientists from the HeartMath Institute studied how one human being can affect the HRV waveforms of other human beings. These experiments consisted of teaching a human being how to maintain higher emotional energies such as love, appreciation, gratitude or peace while the human being functioned within a group. Even though only one member of the group was intentionally focused on higher emotional energies, after a short period of time, all members of the group began to function at higher emotional energies. As a result, group communication improved, fewer mistakes were made, productivity increased, creativity increased and better decisions were made.

I have one more example that combines management of the heart brain with the concept of critical mass. In 1982, Israel was at war with Lebanon. Using meditation techniques, researchers trained subjects to focus on the higher frequency emotional energy of peace in their heart brains. At appointed times, on specific days, these subjects were positioned throughout the war area in the Middle East. During the time these subjects were meditating to focus on peace, all terrorist activities ceased, police reported a decrease in crimes and traffic accidents and hospital personnel reported decreased emergency room visits.

After this experiment, scientists predicted the number of people that would need to focus on peace in order to affect a larger group (critical mass). For a city of one million people, there would need to be 100 people and for a world of 6 billion people, there would need to be 8,000 people. Scientists also predicted that if the number of people focusing on peace was above critical mass, the change in the surrounding areas would be faster.

Let us recap. The human body has a cranial brain and a heart brain. These two brains communicate with each other through the autonomic nervous system. The heart brain responds to the emotional energies of the human being and adjusts the HRV waveform of the heart. The HRV waveform is transferred to the amygdala and then sent to the upper brain. Lower frequency emotional energies (fear, anger, anxiety, hate, etcetera) create chaotic HRV waveforms, lower level cortical thinking and send a physiological response to increase stress hormones. Higher frequency emotional energies (love, compassion, appreciation, gratitude, peace, etcetera) create harmonized HRV waveforms, higher level cortical thinking and send a physiological response to decrease stress hormones.

Now that you know that you have a heart brain and that your emotional energy frequency within the heart brain influences your HRV waveform, your cortical thinking and your stress physiology, you have a choice between managing your emotional energy frequency or allowing your environment to control your emotional energy frequency. Managing your emotional energy frequency will require a change in behavior.

Human beings do not like change. If given a choice between continuing a harmful behavior and changing to a new, beneficial behavior, people will often choose to continue the harmful behavior. The harmful behavior is familiar. Change involves the unknown. Even if the change is for the better, people still fear the unknown.

Therefore, think of this change in behavior to manage your heart brain as a 30-day trial. If you do not like the results, you can return to allowing your environment to control your emotional energy frequency.

The first step in managing your heart brain is to learn what it "feels" like to have a harmonized HRV waveform. The goal of the first step is to recognize the difference between "feeling" lower frequency emotional energies and "feeling" higher frequency emotional energies. If you are not managing your heart brain, your HRV waveform is chaotic most of the time; therefore, you already know what lower frequency emotional energies "feel" like and this feeling is normal for you.

In order to create higher frequency emotional energies in your heart brain, your physical body must feel safe. If your energy body feels unsafe or your physical body is in immediate danger, your cranial brain and your heart brain must focus on the lower frequency energies that will keep you alive. If you are not in immediate danger, you can send a signal from your cranial brain to your heart brain and to your adrenal glands that your energy body and physical body are safe. This signal involves deep breathing. Therefore, start by taking three deep breaths and slow the rate of your breathing. As you slow the rate of your breathing, you are communicating to your adrenal glands and your heart brain that you are safe.

Once your energy body feels safe, you can use your cranial brain to visualize something that makes you feel a higher emotional energy (love, compassion, joy, happiness, appreciation, gratitude, peace, etcetera). This visualization can be a pet that loves you, a grandchild, a spouse, a child, a friend or a stranger that was kind to you. Focus on how your visualizations make you feel. You are looking for visualizations that make you feel happy, that make you smile or that make your heart feel warm or relaxed. Find the visualizations that create a feeling of love, joy or peace. These visualizations will be your higher emotional energy triggers.

I find it more effective when my visualizations have some action. Instead of visualizing my dog, I visualize my dog jumping into my lap or walking along side of me. Similarly, instead of visualizing the ocean, I visualize walking along the beach with my best friend. Once you have your higher emotional energy triggers, try adding some action that makes you feel loved, happy or at peace.

The second step in managing your heart brain is to use your higher emotional energy triggers to harmonize your heart's HRV waveforms on a regular basis. When you wake up in the morning, take three deep breaths and visualize your higher emotional energy triggers at the same time. Maybe you can set the timer on your phone to go off every 30 minutes. Every 30 minutes, you take three slow, deep breaths and visualize your higher emotional energy triggers at the same time. This activity will take 15 seconds and is just a suggestion.

Remember you have free will, so choose whatever reminders and schedule you like.

Sometime during this 30-day trial, your higher emotional energies will begin to feel normal. When your energy body receives lower frequency emotional energies from your environment, these lower frequency emotional energies will be received by your heart chakra.

Your heart brain will identify the chaotic HRV waveforms as abnormal. The heart brain will send this chaotic waveform to your amygdala. Your amygdala will relay this chaotic HRV waveform to your cortical brain and you will identify this lower frequency emotional feeling as abnormal. You will take a deep breath and visualize your higher emotional energy triggers. Your cranial brain will send a signal to your heart brain to increase the frequency of the emotional energy received through your heart chakra. Your heart brain will send the higher frequency emotional energies to your heart, your HRV waveform will harmonize and the lower frequency emotional energy received by your energy body will be blocked from entering your energy fields.

The third step in managing your heart brain is to use your harmonized HRV waveforms to influence other lifeforms. I recommend you start with your pet, if you have one. Your pet's HRV waveforms will synchronize with your HRV waveforms. If your HRV waveforms are harmonized while you are in the presence of your pet, your pet's HRV waveforms will harmonize.

If you are still driving, you can use your harmonized HRV waveforms to influence other drivers. After you start the car, take a deep breath and visualize your higher emotional energy triggers. Practice taking a deep breath and visualizing your higher emotional energy triggers whenever another driver irritates you. Eventually, you will notice that you are calmer while driving and other drivers will stop irritating you. You will also notice that the other drivers will be more courteous.

If you go shopping, you can use your harmonized HRV waveforms to influence other shoppers. As you enter the store, take a deep breath and visualize your higher emotional energy triggers. Try to maintain a harmonized HRV waveform as you walk through the store. Then pay attention to the other customers. Your presence will make them happier, more courteous and more helpful.

I think you get the idea. Try maintaining a harmonized HRV waveform at home with your family and see if your family communication improves. In addition, try maintaining a harmonized HRV waveform at work, school, church or any other group encounter. Then pay attention to how the individuals in the group perform.

Managing Your Anxiety

No matter how prepared you are for the upcoming evolutionary shift, you will experience some anxiety before, during and after the shift.

During the evolutionary shift, human beings will experience a change in physical form and evolve into the unknown. Any major change involving the unknown creates anxiety.

Anxiety creates a chaotic HRV wave form. This chaotic HRV wave form is sent to the amygdala via the heart brain. The amygdala interprets this chaotic waveform as fear and sends the lower frequency emotional energy of fear to the cranial brain. The cranial brain waveform becomes chaotic and the cranial brain sends a signal to the adrenal glands to increase stress hormones.

Your ability to function decreases when you have anxiety. Communication becomes less effective and your ability to make decisions decreases dramatically. In addition, the lower frequency emotional energy of fear decreases your productivity and decreases your creativity which decreases your ability to solve problems.

Your preparation for the evolutionary shift will be more effective if you manage your anxiety. In addition, you will be less likely to panic if you focus on managing your anxiety during the three-day shift event.

Managing your anxiety involves managing your heart brain and using a simple manual technique. These techniques are not designed to substitute for anxiety supplements or anxiety prescription medication. Those of you who are taking anxiety supplements or anxiety prescription medications should continue to take these supplements or medications.

The first step in managing your anxiety is to manage your heart brain. You learned how to manage your heart brain in the previous section. If you choose to manage your heart brain, you can manage your anxiety during the same 30-day trial.

The second step in managing your anxiety is to use a simple manual technique. Place one hand over your heart brain and one hand and forearm across the upper abdomen, just under the rib cage. Close your eyes and visualize your adrenal glands coming into your lower hand and forearm. Then visualize your heart brain connecting to your adrenal glands.

In an earlier chapter, you learned that when two electrical entities are connected, the entity with the lower energy frequency will resonate with the entity that has the higher energy frequency. In this case, your adrenal glands have the lower frequency emotional energy of fear and your heart brain has the higher frequency emotional energies.

The manual connection with your hands will encourage the emotional energy in your adrenal glands to resonate with the emotional energies in your heart brain. Your anxiety will decrease as the emotional energy in your adrenal glands changes from fear to the higher emotional energies you created in your heart brain.

Managing Emotional Shock

Before I present how to manage emotional shock, I want to explain the difference between physical shock and emotional shock. Most people are familiar with physical shock.

Physical shock is a sudden drop in blood flow throughout the physical body. This sudden drop in blood flow is related to severe physical trauma (severe burns, severe infection, severe wounds, etcetera).

Immediate treatment involves laying the person down, raising the legs and calling 911.

Emotional shock is a sudden detachment from all emotional energies. This detachment is related to severe emotional trauma. Sometimes when a human being experiences or observes a severe emotional trauma, the human being is unable to manage the magnitude of lower frequency emotional energies received by the heart chakra. These lower frequency emotional energies are sent to the amygdala via the heart brain. The amygdala interprets these lower frequency emotional energies as extreme fear and extreme anxiety. The amygdala's chaotic waveform is relayed to the cranial brain which has difficulty managing the magnitude of lower frequency emotional energies. Therefore, the cranial brain sends out two signals. One signal goes to the adrenal glands to increase stress hormones. The second signal goes to the kidneys to stop normal kidney movement.

Stopping normal kidney movement effectively shuts down the human being's emotional energy system.

Human beings with emotional shock feel detached and withdrawn from the physical world. They are unable to feel any emotional energies. They cannot feel sad, angry, love or happy. These human beings have difficulty communicating, cannot make good decisions and are not able to problem solve.

Emotional shock will be a major problem during the upcoming evolutionary shift. Human beings who do not prepare for the evolutionary shift will become frightened on the first day of the evolutionary shift. Some will believe that the world is ending when the sun and the moon stop moving. Other human beings will experience emotional shock when they hear or see on the news that four major cities have collapsed into the ocean on the second day of the evolutionary shift. Emotional shock will be rampant on the third day of the evolutionary shift. Even some human beings who prepared for the evolutionary shift will experience emotional shock when they see other human beings and animals disappear. Similarly, some human beings who prepared for the evolutionary shift and who evolve to fourth dimensional form will experience emotional shock when they observe other human beings struggle in third dimensional form.

If you learn to manage your heart brain to harmonize your HRV waveforms and manage your anxiety, you will be able to manage your emotional shock during the upcoming evolutionary shift. The manual technique that will help you pull yourself out of emotional shock is similar to the manual technique used to manage your anxiety.

You will know that you have emotional shock when you cannot feel any emotional energies in your heart brain. You will not feel fear or anxiety and your emotional energy triggers will not create a happy or loving feeling.

If this happens, find your left collarbone. Just below the left collarbone, you will find your first rib. Count down to the third rib and move your finger toward your breast bone until you are at the junction between the third rib and the breast bone. Your finger will be over your aortic valve. Now place your right finger over the aortic valve and the palm of your righthand over your heart. Place your left hand and forearm over the top of your abdomen, just below the rib cage (the same hand placement that is used for managing your anxiety).

You have neurons (cranial brain cells) located at your aortic valve. These aortic valve neurons are dedicated to managing your kidney health which includes your kidney movement. With your hands in the previous positions, visualize your kidneys connecting to your left hand and forearm and begin deep breathing. You will know that your kidneys are beginning to move again when you are able to feel fear or anxiety. When you begin to feel lower frequency emotional energies (fear and anxiety), you know that you are beginning to recover from your emotional shock.

Keep your hands in the same place but change your visualization. Visualize the neurons at your aortic valve connecting to the right finger and your heart brain connecting to the palm of your right hand. Then visualize both your kidneys and your adrenal glands connecting to your left hand and forearm. Now use your emotional energy triggers to harmonize your HRV waveforms until you feel happy and peaceful.

Emotional shock is rare, so you may not have a chance to use the preceding technique until the evolutionary shift. You can prepare by practicing the hand placements and visualizations once a day until this technique becomes automatic.

Karmic Energies

If your truth recognizes karmic energy, I recommend that you clear your karmic fear energies that will prevent your embodiment from evolving to fourth dimensional form when Earth begins to evolve to fourth dimensional form during the upcoming evolutionary shift. Your karmic energies are part of your soul's journey.

Your soul's journey began when your soul was created. The primary goal for your soul is to evolve and emulate your Creator. Although your Creator holds all energies, your Creator is primarily higher frequency emotional energies (love, compassion, hope, peace, etcetera).

To evolve, your soul has been sending part of itself to Earth school and attaching itself to embodiments for thousands of years. Your soul and embodiments learn lessons during each life time. When your embodiment dies, the part of your soul attached to your embodiment returns to your soul. Your soul and your Creator review the lessons that your soul learned. The lessons that your soul did not learn during each lifetime become part of your soul's karmic energies. The unlearned lessons are repeated in a subsequent life time.

Initially, your soul's lessons revolved around tribal rules and tribal survival. In this lifetime, you belong to various tribes. Your family is a tribe. Many of you belong to a work tribe and a religious tribe.

Children belong to a school tribe and perhaps a sports tribe or a scout tribe. Each tribe has its own beliefs, expectations, traditions and prejudices.

The primary goal of any tribe is group survival. In order to survive, each tribe develops rules that the members of the tribe are expected to follow. When a tribal member does not follow the rules, tribal punishment is enacted.

In your past lives, one form of tribal punishment was abandonment. When tribes consisted of twenty people, abandonment meant death. Early human beings could not survive without the support of the tribe. Whenever a tribe excluded a member from the tribe because the member did not follow the rules, the tribal member developed the fear of abandonment. This fear of tribal abandonment is one of your karmic energies.

Other forms of punishment included physical and emotional abuse. All of you experienced some form of physical and emotional abuse in your past lives. Whenever a tribe abused a tribal member, the tribal member developed a fear of tribal punishment. The fear of tribal punishment is one of your karmic energies.

Tribal punishment centers on the theme that the tribal member is not doing things well enough for the tribe. For example, in this lifetime, children belonging to a sports tribe may not be allowed to play during competition because they do not do things well enough during practice. Adults may not receive a raise from their employer because they do not do things well enough for the work tribe. All of you experienced tribal punishment in your past lives. Whenever a tribe withheld a reward or distributed punishment, the tribal member developed the fear of not doing things well enough for the tribe. The fear of not doing things well enough for the tribe is one of your karmic energies.

Tribes focused on survival will prioritize tribal needs over individual needs. The individuals within the tribe will create the fear that they are unimportant to the tribe because their individual needs are not being met. For example, when children do not receive the attention they need to thrive, they begin to believe that they are unimportant to the family tribe. Similarly, when employees are ignored, or receive negative feedback from their employers, they begin to believe that they are unimportant to the work tribe. All of you have experienced the fear of being unimportant to a tribe in your past lives. The fear of being unimportant to a tribe is one of your karmic energies.

Tribal fears have an emotional energy frequency that correlates with the first chakra. These tribal fears are received by the first chakra and stored in the physical energy field. All of you have these four karmic energies stored in your physical energy field.

At some point, your soul began working on lessons revolving around individual relationships with other human beings. Your soul also worked on individual relationships with animals, food, alcohol, drugs, money and sex. For the last thirty-five thousand years, your relationship lessons have focused on control.

All of you have experienced difficult lifetimes. During these difficult lifetimes, your embodiments were controlled by circumstances such as war, slavery, poverty or disease. In addition, you experienced lifetimes where other human beings controlled your embodiments with physical abuse or sexual abuse. Similarly, you experienced lifetimes where other human beings controlled your embodiment's energy body with verbal abuse, verbal intimidation and verbal criticism.

When life's circumstances are difficult, most human beings try to escape the earthly experience. One way to escape the negative control circumstances around you is to develop addictive relationships with food, alcohol, nicotine or other drugs. The great experiment in the twentieth century was to use food as a way to escape negative circumstances. Overeating sugar, chocolate and foods high in fat helped many of you escape negative circumstances.

All of these relationship lessons related to being controlled by other people, money, sex and addictive substances created the fear of being controlled. This fear of being controlled is one of your karmic energies.

In an attempt to learn the relationship lesson that people cannot be controlled, you have all tried to control others in your past lives. You have all experienced lifetimes where you controlled other human beings with physical abuse or sexual abuse. Similarly, you have all experienced lifetimes where you controlled the energy bodies of other human beings with verbal abuse, verbal intimidation and verbal criticism.

In addition to trying to control other human beings, souls have been learning relationship lessons about controlling circumstances. These lessons included trying to control the environment, animals and life events.

All of these relationship lessons related to trying to control human beings, circumstances, money, sex and addictions created the fear that you cannot control. The fear that you cannot control is one of your karmic energies.

The only true constant in your past lives has been change. Change has not always been positive. Negative change included losing love ones to war and disease, being sold into slavery or forcing you into an abusive relationship. All of you have karmic energies related to the fear of change.

Relationship energies have an emotional energy frequency that correlates with the second chakra. These three control fears (fear of being controlled, fear that you cannot control and fear of change) are received by the second chakra and stored in the unconscious energy field. All of you have these three karmic energies stored in your unconscious energy field.

All of you have experienced survival issues in your past lives. Many of you experienced violent deaths related to war or physical violence.

Similarly, many of you experienced survival issues related to disease or poverty. During these lifetimes, you developed the fear that you would not physically or emotionally survive. This fear that you will not survive is one of your karmic energies.

In addition, all of you have experienced past lives where you were criticized for not doing things well enough. This criticism developed the fear of not being perfect. This fear that you are not perfect is one of your karmic energies.

The two preceding karmic energies (fear of survival and fear of not being perfect) are related to your personal power energies. Personal power also relates to personal safety, self-esteem and self-respect. These personal power emotional energies have an emotional frequency that correlates with the third chakra. The third chakra receives these personal power energies and stores these energies in the emotional energy field. All of you have these two personal power karmic energies stored in your emotional energy field.

Your soul's lessons over the last thirty-five thousand years placed a tremendous strain on your embodiments' heart chakra and heart brain. Many of your embodiments experienced brutal tribal wars, slavery and persecution. Several of your embodiments were abused physically and emotionally. These negative experiences created tribal fears, relationship fears focused on control and survival fears that entered your embodiments through the heart chakra. This constant bombardment of lower frequency fears kept your embodiments' heart brain in a chaotic HRV wave form. Unable to harmonize the HRV wave form, your embodiments' heart brain was unable to increase the frequency of emotional energy in the embodiments' heart chakra. Therefore, the embodiments' heart chakra absorbed emotional wounds and created the fear that these wounds would never heal. In addition, the constant chaotic HRV energy wave forms created the fear that your embodiments could not protect themselves emotionally. Maintaining a constant chaotic HRV energy wave form depleted your embodiments' emotional resources and created the fear that your embodiment did not have enough emotional energy.

When your emotional energy was low and your embodiment felt wounded, your embodiment created the fear that your Creator abandoned you.

All four of these fears (your emotional wounds would not heal, you could not protect yourself emotionally, you did not have enough emotional energy and your Creator abandoned you) are karmic energies. These four karmic energies have an emotional energy frequency that correlates with the fourth chakra. Your soul brought these four karmic energies forward in this lifetime so that they would be received by the fourth chakra and stored in your psyche energy field. All of you have these four karmic energies stored in your psyche energy field.

Working on lessons related to control over several life times has placed a strain on the human ego. During lifetimes where the embodiment was intimidated and criticized, the ego created the fears that it was not good enough and not worthy enough. Unfortunately, these lessons related to control often resulted in physical violence. In an attempt to control others, the human embodiment experienced war, slavery and physical abuse. In response to these traumatic events, the human ego created the fear that it would be energetically destroyed.

All three of these fears (you are not good enough, you are not worthy enough and you will be energetically destroyed) are karmic energies. These ego karmic energies have an emotional frequency that correlates with the fifth chakra. These karmic energies were brought forward in this lifetime, received by your fifth chakra and stored in your ego energy field. All of you have these three karmic energies stored in your ego energy field.

Experiencing so much physical violence over several lifetimes created a dilemma for your embodiments. The part of your soul connected to your embodiments knew that the Creator existed and that the primary emotional energy for the Creator is love. However, the amount of intimidation, criticism and physical violence experienced by your embodiments created the fear that your Creator did not exist, love did not exist and you were damned.

The preceding three fears (the Creator does not exist, love does not exist and you are damned) are karmic energies. The fears related to the Creator and to love have an emotional frequency that correlates with the sixth chakra. The fear that you are damned has the emotional frequency that correlates with the seventh chakra. These karmic energies were brought forward in this lifetime, received by the sixth and seventh chakras and stored in your subconscious and mental energy fields.

The karmic energies located within your auric energy field come from more than one chakra. All of you have three karmic energies located in your auric energy field.

The first karmic energy located within your auric energy field came from the first three chakras. When you were punished for not doing things well enough for the tribe (first chakra), you began to judge yourself as not being perfect (third chakra). This fear that you were not perfect was reinforced by the criticism of others (second chakra). In addition, you learned to criticize others who did not do things well enough for you.

The combination of criticizing others (second chakra) for not doing things well enough for you (first chakra) resulted in the judgment of others. The combination of receiving criticism (second chakra) for not doing things well enough (first chakra) and for not being perfect (third chakra) resulted in self-judgment.

All of you have self-judgment as a karmic energy within your auric energy field. Your willingness to judge others is based on your willingness to judge yourself in a negative manner.

The second karmic energy located within your auric energy field came from the first four chakras. When you were abandoned or punished for not doing things well enough (first chakra), you developed despair. Similarly, when people, money, sex, addictive substances and circumstances controlled you (second chakra), you developed despair. Likewise, when you feared for your survival and you believed that you were not perfect (third chakra), you developed despair. Your despair created the fear that your Creator abandoned you (fourth chakra). All of you have the karmic energy that your Creator abandoned you in your auric energy field.

The third karmic energy located within your auric energy field was created when your embodiments' belief conflicted with your soul's belief. Your soul believed that the ultimate goal for learning lessons on Earth was to move toward love and compassion and this ultimate goal was consistent with the will of your Creator. Therefore, all earthly lessons created by your soul were designed to follow the Creator's will.

Unfortunately, your lifetime of lessons related to control included tribal abandonment and tribal punishment (first chakra), control and criticism (second chakra), sudden and violent deaths (third chakra) and emotional wounds (fourth chakra). These painful lives created the fear that if you follow the will of your Creator, you will be destroyed (fifth chakra). All of you have the karmic energy that if you follow the will of your Creator, you will be destroyed in your auric energy field.

Let us recap. Your soul has been working on lessons related to control for thousands of years. During this lifetime, your soul has brought forward karmic energies that need to be cleared so your embodiment can evolve from third dimensional form to fourth dimensional form.

These karmic energies are stored in the following energy fields:

> Physical energy field: tribal karmic fears
>> Fear of abandonment
>> Fear of punishment
>> Fear of not doing things well enough
>> Fear of being unimportant
> Unconscious energy field: relationship karmic fears
>> Fear of being controlled
>> Fear of not being able to control
>> Fear of change

Emotional energy field: personal power karmic fears

> Fear of survival
>
> Fear of not being perfect

Psyche energy field: emotional power karmic fears

> Fear of abandonment
>
> Fear that you cannot protect yourself emotionally
>
> Fear that your emotional wounds will not heal
>
> Fear that you do not have enough emotional energy

Ego energy field: ego karmic fears

> Fear of not being good enough
>
> Fear of not being worthy enough
>
> Fear of being energetically destroyed

Subconscious energy field: spiritual karmic fears

> Fear that your Creator does not exist
>
> Fear that love does not exist

Mental energy field: spiritual karmic fears

> Fear that you are damned

Auric energy field

> Self -judgment
>
> Fear that your Creator abandoned you
>
> Fear that if you follow the will of your Creator, you
> will be destroyed

Healing Tools

When the Creator created souls to manage and learn on Earth, the Creator created healing tools for the evolution of these souls. The five healing tools needed for clearing your karmic energies are the healing icosahedron, light beings, the angelic realm, your Balanced Healing Team and nature essences.

Icosahedron

The icosahedron is a healing grid formed by your Creator to help you heal your energy body and your physical body (Fig 3). This healing grid is in the tenth dimension, so human beings who are in the third dimension cannot see it. Your soul passes through the healing icosahedron every time a part of your soul comes down to Earth school.

The icosahedron on this page (Fig 3) represents the healing icosahedron. I recommend that you draw a blue circle in the center representing Earth. Then take a green highlighter and trace around all of the solid lines. Your soul will recognize and remember passing though this healing energy field on the way to Earth.

Up until three thousand years ago, the ancient people on Earth used the healing icosahedron for healing. Unfortunately, three thousand years ago the people on Earth entered a very dark period of time. Anger, fear and physical violence dominated Earth and the information about the healing icosahedron was lost.

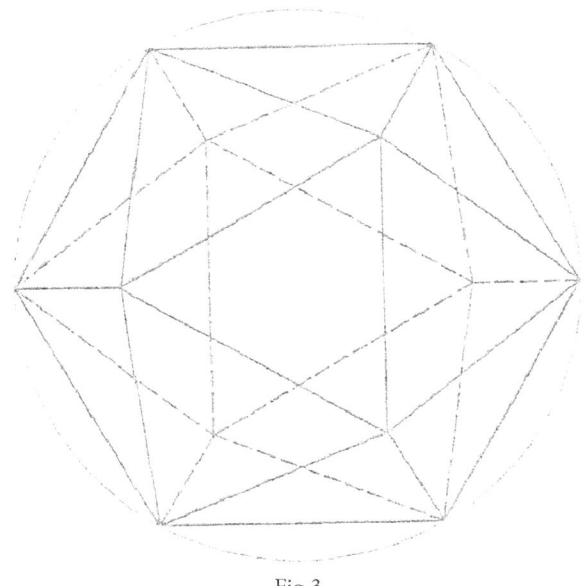

Fig 3

Light Beings

The Creator created light beings to help all physical forms on Earth. Every human being has a deva of form and a nature spirit of form. The deva of form is responsible for the human being's genetics. All of the characteristics of the physical form are held by the deva of form. The nature spirit of form is responsible for implementing any changes designed by the deva of form.

For example, if you decide to overeat on a regular basis, the deva of form will establish a blueprint for a heavier physical body. This blueprint will be given to the nature spirit of form who will help you increase your amount of fat tissue. This fat tissue will be placed according to the blueprint created by your deva of form. Some of you will increase abdominal fat first while others will increase fat tissue around the hips and thighs first.

Similarly, if you decide to eat less and exercise to lose weight, your deva of form will establish a blueprint for a thinner body. This blueprint will be given to your nature spirit of form who will help you decrease the amount of fat tissue. Where you lose fat tissue first will be determined by the blueprint created by your deva of form.

Your deva of form and your nature spirit of form will help you establish a healing icosahedron around your physical form so that you can connect with the healing icosahedron that surrounds Earth. These two light beings will help you clear your karmic energies. When you decide to clear your karmic energies, your deva of form will create a blueprint for clearing the karmic energies and your nature spirit of form will use this blueprint and clear the karmic energies out of your energy fields.

The third light being that will help you clear your karmic energies is Pan. Pan is the chief executive officer for all nature spirits. This light being has the power to change the lower frequency fear energies removed from your energy fields to higher frequency love energies. Pan will send the higher frequency love energies to your deva of form. The deva of form will provide a blueprint for your nature spirit of form and your nature spirit of form will use these higher frequency love energies to heal your energy fields.

Angelic Realm

The Creator created the angelic realm to support the souls that come down to Earth school and the embodiments that the souls attach to. The angels have a specific vibration designed to help the evolution of Earth beings through healing, guidance and protection.

Angels are divided into groups based on function and each group has two Archangel leaders. An Archangel of Healing will help you establish your healing icosahedron so you can connect to the healing icosahedron that surrounds Earth. When you decide to clear your karmic energies that will prevent you from evolving to fourth dimensional form, the Archangel of Healing will identify these karmic energies and send this information to your deva of form. Your deva of form will create a blueprint for clearing these karmic energies and send this blueprint to your nature spirit of form. After Pan increases the emotional energy frequency of the fear energies removed from your energy fields to a higher emotional energy frequency of love, the Archangel of Healing will provide additional higher frequency love energy and determine where all of this love energy will be applied in your energy fields. The Archangel of Healing will send this information to your deva of form who will develop a blueprint for healing your energy fields. This blueprint will be sent to your nature spirit of form.

Balanced Healing Team

Your Balanced Healing Team consists of five entities: the part of your soul attached to your embodiment, the Archangel of Healing, Pan, your deva of form and your nature spirit of form. Remember that you have been given free will. This team will not function unless you choose to work with them. You must ask them to come and take their places around your physical form if you choose to work with them.

When you decide to clear your karmic energies that will prevent you from evolving to fourth dimensional form, you will ask the members of your Balanced Healing Team to come and take their places at their five points. Pan is always at your head. Your soul is always on your left. The Archangel of Healing is always on your right. Your deva of form is always at your right foot and your nature spirit of form is always at your left foot.

Nature Essences

Nature essences are healing energies that come from flowers. The best example I have is Rescue Remedy. Rescue Remedy is made up of five nature essences. The combination of these nature essences decreases the lower frequency fear energy related to anxiety. When I become anxious and I am unable to quickly increase the frequency of this anxiety energy with my heart brain, I add 2-3 drops of Rescue Remedy to my water or tea. I drink liquids with Rescue Remedy all day or until my anxiety is gone.

The Creator created nature essences to help heal the energy fields of all living beings. These essences have a specific energy frequency that matches a specific energy field.

After you have cleared your karmic energies and replaced these energies with higher frequency love energies, you will ask your Balanced Healing

Team to continue healing your energy fields. Nature essences will help with this continued healing process.

I will use an open wound analogy to explain. If new skin covers an open wound before the wound is healed, a cavity develops between the bottom of the wound and the skin. This cavity will fill with fluid and become infected. That is why a wound care technician will remove the dead tissue and any new premature tissue to allow the wound to heal from the inside out. The wound care technician will clean the wound and apply whatever medication has been prescribed to assist with the healing process.

Using this analogy, you will ask your Balanced Healing Team to interweave the new higher frequency love energy with the healing energies that have the appropriate color, tone and geometry needed to heal the energy hole created by clearing your karmic energies. You will then ask your Balanced Healing Team to clean and reseal the area with healing energies that have the appropriate color, tone and geometry. Your request to strengthen and restore the energy fields will include adding nature essences. Your deva of form will work with the deva of forms for all the appropriate nature essences and place these healing energies into your blueprint for healing the energy fields.

Clearing Your Karma

You will begin by establishing your healing icosahedron and clearing all of your chakras. Think of your chakras as your plumbing system. Your karmic energies will flow out of the energy field into the attached chakra, down the pranic tube into the third chakra. All of your karmic fear energies will drain out of your body through your third chakra. Your Balanced Healing Team will create an emerald green energy tube that will extend from the third chakra to the healing icosahedron that surrounds Earth and extends down into Earth five feet. At five feet, the nature spirits, under the direction of Pan, can easily clean up the lower frequency emotional fear energy and increase this emotional energy to love energy.

When you are ready, read the following:

"Dear Balanced Healing Team, please come and take your places at your five points.

Please establish the emerald green icosahedron around my form so that I can connect to the healing grid that surrounds Earth.

Please activate the flow of healing from the healing grid that surrounds Earth to the healing grid that surrounds my form.

Please clear all of the karmic energies that will prevent me from evolving to fourth dimensional form out of

The third chakra down the emerald green tube into the earth five feet. I ask that the nature spirits clean up this energy, upgrade the frequency and recycle this energy back through Pan, into me, to be used for a higher purpose.

The second and fourth chakras, down the pranic tube into the third chakra, down the emerald green tube into the earth five feet. I ask that the nature spirits clean up this energy, upgrade the frequency and recycle this energy back through Pan, into me, to be used for a higher purpose.

The first and fifth chakras, down the pranic tube into the third chakra, down the emerald green tube into the earth five feet. I ask that the nature spirits clean up this energy, upgrade the frequency and recycle this energy back through Pan, into me, to be used for a higher purpose.

The sixth and seventh chakras, down the pranic tube into the third chakra, down the emerald green tube into the earth five feet. I ask that the nature spirits clean up this energy, upgrade the frequency and recycle this energy back through Pan, into me, to be used for a higher purpose.

The physical energy field into the first chakra, down the pranic tube into the third chakra, down the emerald green tube into the earth five feet. I ask that the nature spirits clean up this energy, upgrade the frequency and recycle this energy back through Pan, into me, to be used for a higher purpose.

The unconscious energy field into the second chakra, down the pranic tube into the third chakra, down the emerald green tube into the earth five feet. I ask that the nature spirits clean up this energy, upgrade the frequency and recycle this energy back through Pan, into me, to be used for a higher purpose.

The emotional energy field into the third chakra, down the emerald green tube into the earth five feet. I ask that the nature spirits clean up this energy, upgrade the frequency and recycle this energy back through Pan, into me, to be used for a higher purpose.

The psych energy field into the fourth chakra, down the pranic tube into the third chakra, down the emerald green tube into the earth five feet. I ask that the nature spirits clean up this energy, upgrade the frequency and recycle this energy back through Pan, into me, to be used for a higher purpose.

The ego energy field into the fifth chakra, down the pranic tube into the third chakra, down the emerald green tube into the earth five feet. I ask that the nature spirits clean up this energy, upgrade the frequency and recycle this energy back through Pan, into me, to be used for a higher purpose.

The subconscious energy field into the sixth chakra, down the pranic tube into the third chakra, down the emerald green tube into the earth five feet. I ask that the nature spirits clean up this energy, upgrade the frequency and recycle this energy back through Pan, into me, to be used for a higher purpose.

The mental energy field into the seventh chakra, down the pranic tube into the third chakra, down the emerald green tube into the earth five feet. I ask that the nature spirits clean up this energy, upgrade the frequency and recycle this energy back through Pan, into me, to be used for a higher purpose.

The auric energy field into the fourth chakra, down the pranic tube into the third chakra, down the emerald green tube into the earth five feet. I ask that the nature spirits clean up this energy, upgrade the frequency and recycle this energy back through Pan, into me, to be used for a higher purpose.

Please interweave all of my chakras and energy fields with the appropriate color, tone and geometry for healing.

Please wash all of my chakras and energy fields with the appropriate color and tone for healing.

Please reseal all of my chakras and energy fields with the appropriate color, tone and geometry for healing.

Please strengthen and restore all of my chakras and energy fields with the appropriate color, tone and geometry for healing. I ask that the devas for the nature essences for all of my chakras and energy fields come and superimpose the complete architectural blueprint for healing on my form.

I close with love and gratitude for the healing you have provided."

Physical Preparation

Things will be a little rocky after the evolutionary shift. Petroleum, fossil fuels, plutonium and uranium will not resonate with Earth's higher electrical energy pulse frequency in the fourth dimensional areas. These materials will be used up quickly. Please do not panic. Scientists know how to produce electricity without these products. It may take six months to a year for all fourth dimensional areas to have electricity for heating and cooling. If you own your home and you have the financial resources, I recommend that you make your home energy independent. The lack of electricity will produce a short-term water shortage and the lack of petroleum will affect transportation. If you have the financial resources, I recommend that you store a six-month supply of food and water for your family.

Initially, only thirty percent of all adults on Earth will evolve to fourth dimensional form. This decrease in population will affect manufacturing. If you have the financial resources, I recommend that you store a one-year supply of dry goods (toilet paper, paper towels, cleaning supplies, etcetera). I also recommend that you store a one-year supply of all supplements.

Please have hope. All of these problems will be resolved during the first year after the evolutionary shift.

A special note to people living in Los Angeles, Washington DC, New York City and Rhome, Italy. If you are preparing for the upcoming evolutionary shift, I recommend you create an exit strategy from these cities. All of these cities will fall into the ocean during the second day of the evolutionary shift. When the news media starts to report that the embodiments of Mother Mary and Quan Yin are seen throughout the world, determine how you will leave these cities and create to go bags for your family. When the sun and moon stop moving during the first day of the evolutionary shift, you must exit these cities immediately. Waiting to leave on the next day will be too late.

AFTER THE
EVOLUTIONARY SHIFT

Community Rebound

Remember that every twenty-six thousand years, Earth's rotation slows down, stops and restarts in the opposite direction. During the past shifts, seventy percent of the human population died. The upcoming evolutionary shift will be different. The Creator wants sixty percent of the human population to survive the evolutionary shift.

All souls coming to Earth school are aware of the upcoming evolutionary shift. Forty percent of these souls volunteered to leave Earth before or during the evolutionary shift. Sixty percent of these souls volunteered to live through the evolutionary shift.

Fifty percent of the people who live after the evolutionary shift will initially remain in third dimensional form. Some of these people will have souls and embodiments who are not ready to evolve. A minority of these people will be prepared to evolve and their souls chose to stay in third dimensional form to help others evolve to fourth dimensional form.

The other fifty percent of the people who live after the evolutionary shift will evolve to fourth dimensional form. Some of these people will be located in fourth dimensional areas and some of these people will be located in third dimensional areas.

On the day after the evolutionary shift, prepared leaders who evolved to fourth dimensional form will identify other people who evolved to fourth dimensional form. These fourth dimensional human beings will be encouraged to gather at a local building. These gatherings will be the beginning of the post evolutionary shift community rebound.

Whether you evolve to fourth dimensional form in a fourth dimensional area or a third dimensional area or you stay in third dimensional form to help others to evolve, you will become part of a community in order to survive the extreme changes that occur after the evolutionary shift. Community goals will vary depending on which dimensional area your physical body is in. In addition, community goals for fourth dimensional individuals will be different than third dimensional individuals.

All people who live after the evolutionary shift will experience anxiety. People unprepared will experience shock, confusion, anxiety and fear. People who prepared for the evolutionary shift will rebound quickly through shock and anxiety. These people will develop a community that will bring hope and guidance to others after the evolutionary shift.

The first goal of the prepared community will be communication. During the initial gatherings, prepared leaders will continue to communicate about Earth changes, individual rebound from shock and anxiety and the need to work together as a community to solve problems.

The first problem for all fourth dimensional human beings will be the rescuing and caring for children who no longer have parents. All children age 10 or younger will evolve to fourth dimensional form.

Eighty percent of the young adults between age 11 and age 18 will evolve to fourth dimensional form. Many parents will die in the earthquakes and transportation accidents during the three-day evolutionary shift, leaving children without parents. Other parents will stay in third dimensional form while their children evolve to fourth dimensional form. Local communities will establish a search and rescue for local children who are alone and without parents.

Community goals for these children will depend on where they are located. Fourth dimensional children located in third dimensional areas will be transported to fourth dimensional areas by the fourth dimensional people who rescued them. In contrast, the communities in the fourth dimensional areas will begin working on solving the problem of temporary care for these children. Temporary foster cares will be established and if necessary, group homes will be established.

Fourth Dimensional Areas – Year One Local Community Rebound

The mental construct for people in fourth dimensional form will include cooperation, compassion and concern for all members of the community. People will understand that they must work together to survive. Individuals will identify their own skills and determine how they will help the local community solve community problems. In addition, individuals will identify their own needs and ask the community for help.

Local governments will develop a partnership between government officials, business owners and community members. Many local community leaders will stay in third dimensional form. Therefore, new local community leaders will be chosen.

Communication will be a primary goal of local leaders. The time of keeping secrets from the people will be over. Local leaders will develop ways to communicate what is happening locally. In addition, a way of receiving community feedback will be developed.

People will rely on local governments, local businesses and community members to provide community services. Basic community services involving communication, transportation, housing, energy for heating, cooling and cooking, waste disposal, food supply, children education and animal care will need to be established.

Business owners and community members will divide into groups and work in areas where they have experience. Some members of the community will work on how to provide energy to the homes, schools, hospitals, businesses in the community and government buildings. Other members of the community will work on how to maintain water, sewage and waste disposal. Community services involving fire and safety will be restructured. Child and young adult education and animal care will be restructured.

Communities will need to establish their initial goals and the vision they have for their community. The fourth dimensional mental construct will be that everyone has a home, everyone works, everyone has enough food, everyone deserves excellent health care and everyone contributes to the community in an area they enjoy and are good at.

People living in fourth dimensional areas will develop new ways to provide electricity to their homes, schools, hospitals, government offices and businesses. In the fourth dimensional areas, materials that do not resonate with Earth's new electrical pulse frequency will disappear. This will include fossil fuels and uranium. Fossil fuels include crude oil (petroleum), coal and natural gas. Presently, fossil fuels are used to produce electricity, gasoline and diesel fuel. Researchers are already developing alternate forms of energy that include solar energy, wind energy and generators that produce energy without fossil fuels.

Local communities will address the need for food supplies. The mental construct will be that everyone will have enough food. This goal will be complicated by the change in fourth dimensional form. Fourth dimensional bodies will no longer tolerate foods that do not resonate with their 13 Hz base frequency.

Fourth dimension humans will only eat fish and eggs for meat protein. The frequency of beef, pork, chicken and turkey products will not resonate with fourth dimensional forms. Therefore, people will no longer eat these meat products. Fourth dimensional beings will continue to eat dairy products (milk, cheese and butter).

The need for vegetables, eggs and dairy products will be identified by local community members. Local communities will develop community gardens. In addition, local farms that produce vegetables, fruits, eggs and dairy products will be supported by community members.

Within the fourth dimensional areas, the focus of the police will change. Fourth dimensional beings will have the mental construct that physical violence will only be used to defend oneself. Physical violence toward other human beings or animals will no longer exist. Police will no longer need to focus on murder, physical assault, rape, physical child abuse or physical animal abuse since these behaviors will no longer exist. Police will focus on helping community members and enforcing laws that will keep community members safe.

After the first week, community members will focus on child and young adult education. Public schools will be restructured with an immediate change in teacher qualifications. Many teachers will die or stay in third dimensional form. Therefore, there will be a severe teacher shortage. People beyond retirement age will fill this shortage.

The age of retirement will be over. Fourth dimension beings will value the experience and knowledge of the elderly. All people will work to contribute to the new society. Elderly individuals will work as guides and teachers in their areas of experience.

During the second week, community members will focus on animal care. Many animal owners will stay in third dimensional form, leaving dogs, cats, horses, farm animals and zoo animals without care.

Community members will develop a plan for taking care of these animals.

Initially, community health care will have limited resources. Many physicians, nurses and other medical personnel will stay in third dimensional form creating a shortage of medical personnel.

Local community leaders will take a community census. The census will focus on the skills and experiences of community members. From the census, local community leaders will identify the skills and experiences that are needed to help the community survive.

After the census, local community leaders will reach out to other community leaders. People will begin to share resources. In addition, people will begin to focus on regional government and regional resources.

Regional Community Rebound

Since many people will not evolve to fourth dimensional form, many regional government jobs will need to be filled. Fourth dimensional individuals will begin to develop a larger regional community that will be a partnership between government officials, business owners and private citizens. Regional community goals and a new regional community vision will develop.

This regional community vision will encompass health care stabilization, economic stabilization, child and young adult education and any other services that will help local communities thrive. The mental construct will be that all people deserve superior health care. Child and young adult education will be restructured.

Health care stabilization will involve a change in focus from the treatment of symptoms to the prevention of disease. The mental constructs of people toward health care will change. People will begin to understand that their physical health depends on their emotional (energy) health.

Physicians will learn about the physical body's energy systems and the healing of these energy systems will become a priority. Exercise and good nutrition will become a part of everyone's lifestyle.

Health care stabilization will involve a restructuring of the current medical services and a restructuring of financial payment for health care services. For example, health industries that presently support karmic diseases (cancer, Parkinson's disease, multiple sclerosis and Alzheimer's disease) will no longer be needed since these diseases will no longer exist. Payment for health care services will be restructured so that all people receive superior health care regardless of economic status. Medical insurance will no longer determine the type of health care provided, since health care insurance companies will no longer exist.

The age of health care insurance companies will be over. Many of the corporate offices for health care insurance companies will be located in third dimensional areas. The money located in third dimensional areas will not be available in the fourth dimensional areas. The decrease in financial funds coupled with the claims related to earthquakes will cause the health care insurance companies to fold.

Economic stabilization will involve a restructuring of goods and services provided and a restructuring of the labor force with many jobs eliminated because they are no longer necessary and new jobs developed. Many industries that presently employ thousands of people will no longer be needed in the fourth dimensional areas. The mental constructs of people will change. Beef, chicken, pork and turkey products will not support fourth dimensional bodies.

Therefore, these industries will no longer be needed. The exception will be eggs. Fourth dimensional forms will eat fish and eggs.

Therefore, egg and fish industries will expand accordingly.

Industries providing petroleum and plastic products will no longer be needed because these products will not exist in the fourth dimensional areas. Alternative ways to create electricity will develop before the evolutionary shift that will help with the transition.

Likewise, a product similar to plastic that can be broken down environmentally will be developed before the evolutionary shift.

The economic system in the fourth dimensional areas will still be based on currency, but there will be a more even distribution of this currency. The mental construct in the fourth dimensional areas will be one of cooperation and partnership. All people will work to provide a better community. No one will be homeless and no one will be without a job. Those who have lost their jobs because the industries they worked for no longer exist will easily find work elsewhere. Since many people will not evolve to fourth dimensional form, many jobs will be available.

Social stabilization will be a major priority during the first year after the evolutionary shift. Many people will be without jobs and homes.

Employers will be prepared to train new employees and people will be amenable to changing careers. The banking industry will restructure mortgage loans so that people will be able to take over mortgages of homes that have been deserted by people who stayed in third dimensional form.

National Community Rebound

Many national community leaders will not evolve to fourth dimensional form. New national leaders will be chosen.

The mental construct of national leaders will be one of service, cooperation and communication. National goals will be restructured and a new national vision will develop. This new national vision will include:

1. Everyone will have a job. The age of retirement will be over.
2. Everyone will have a home. The age of homeless people will be over.

3. Everyone will have enough food. The age of starving children will be over.

4. Everyone will have excellent health care. The age of providing excellent health care for some and poor health care for others will be over.

National leaders will focus on mass migration, national health care, economic stabilization, energy production, child, young adult and adult education, food distribution, transportation, national communication and national defense. National government will become a partnership between government officials, business owners and private citizens.

Migration

During the first week following the evolutionary shift there will be a mass migration of people. This migration will be managed by national governments.

National fourth dimensional leaders will help facilitate the movement of people in and out of the fourth dimensional areas. People who evolve to fourth dimensional form and are located in third dimensional areas will have difficulty surviving if they stay in the third dimensional areas. These individuals will not be able to interact with people who are still in third dimensional form. They will lose their social and economic support. To survive, they will migrate to a fourth dimensional area.

In addition, many parents in the third dimensional areas will stay in third dimensional form. These parents will not be able to see their children, leaving thousands of children without parental care. These children will need to be found and moved to a fourth dimensional area.

National governments will establish refugee camps on the border between fourth dimensional and third dimensional areas. Local communities and businesses will communicate with national leaders. The specific skill and experience needed for each community and business will be provided. People migrating to fourth dimensional areas will decide where they want to live and what job they would like to have. They will be recruited by communities and businesses who need their expertise and experience. Everyone will be needed.

Everyone will be wanted.

Children without parents will be initially placed in foster care. National governments will store each child's DNA. Many parents will evolve to fourth dimensional form over the next three years. These parents will be reunited with their children by matching their DNA with their child's DNA.

National Health Care

Payment for healthcare will be a priority for national leaders in fourth dimensional areas. Insurance companies for health care will no longer exist. Payment for medical services will be initially restructured and all fourth dimensional areas will move toward national health insurance.

Economic Stabilization

Businesses that exist after the evolutionary shift will develop partnerships with local, regional and national governments. These partnerships will develop new national goals designed to improve the economy, increase jobs and encourage new businesses.

In addition, businesses with develop partnerships with their employees. Employees will become involved in developing business goals. Business owners will rely on employee feedback on how to improve work conditions and how to accomplish business goals.

Business owners will become invested in the emotional and physical health of their employees. In addition, businesses will provide superior, educational child care environments for the children of their employees.

Energy Production

Researchers will develop sustainable alternative energy before the evolutionary shift that will help with the transition after the evolutionary shift. These alternative energy sources will be important since fossil fuels and uranium will not resonate with Earth's electrical pulse and will not exist.

National leaders will receive feedback from local and regional communities on where these alternative energy sources are needed. Businesses that provide these alternative energy sources will work with national leaders to provide energy to all areas within the fourth dimensional areas.

Education

Initially after the evolutionary shift, national leaders will focus on child and young adult education. Colleges and universities will be shut down.

People in fourth dimensional areas will develop a new vision for childhood education. This vision will begin at the local community level. Local community representatives will be chosen to work at the regional level to develop regional educational goals. Once regional education goals are developed, regional representatives will be chosen to work at the national level. A new national educational vision and new educational goals will develop.

Food Distribution

National leaders will receive feedback from local and regional communities on where food is needed. Local communities will lead the way with local gardens and small farms. Businesses producing food and transporting food products will be supported by national governments.

National Defense

People in fourth dimensional form will believe that physical violence toward other human beings and animals is not a viable behavior.

National leaders will no longer try to control other fourth dimensional areas using physical force.

National leaders in fourth dimensional areas will begin to work with each other on a global defense. This global defense will be needed to defend the fourth dimensional areas from leaders in the third dimensional areas.

Global Community Rebound

National leaders in fourth dimensional areas will communicate with each other within the first month after the evolutionary shift, providing feedback on what is working and what is not working in their areas.

The era of national isolationism will be over. A new global community will form.

Global leaders will work on establishing a global economy and a global defense. This global defense will focus on dismantling the nuclear and conventional bombs in the third dimensional areas.

Let us recap. All fourth dimensional communities, local, regional, national and global will have intelligent beings that hold the key to solving community problems. Everyone will contribute to helping the community by leading in areas of their experience. Everyone will work and share in ways that will make life's responsibilities easier.

Everyone will be involved and everyone will be valued.

Communities will communicate with each other and provide feedback on what is working and what is not working for their areas. Citizens will be involved with local leadership. Local leadership will become involved with regional leadership. Regional leadership will cooperate and assist national leadership. A new global community will evolve.

Self-reliance will become the new normal. Self-reliance is when people live and learn from others. People will offer their strengths and skills to others and integrate the strengths and skills from others to thrive. The era of living with autonomy will be over.

Third Dimensional Areas – Year One

People who prepared for the evolutionary shift will begin communicating to the people who remained in third dimensional form the first day after the evolutionary shift. They will teach about Earth's changes, explain the vanishings into fourth dimensional form, explain that the children will be rescued by other fourth dimensional forms and the potential of being reunited with their loved ones, if they evolve to fourth dimensional form.

Prepared community members will teach how to rebound from shock and anxiety and how to form a community of people preparing to evolve.

In addition, prepared individuals will instruct others to migrate to third dimensional areas. Millions of people who stay in third dimensional form will be located in fourth dimensional areas at the time of the evolutionary shift. These people will not be able to see plants or animals. They will be able to see and manipulate inanimate objects. To survive, these people will migrate to third dimensional areas.

Remember that all embodiments have free will. Some people will begin to move toward a higher base energy frequency of love, compassion and peace. Other people will continue to function at a lower base energy frequency of fear, control and physical violence.

Community rebound after the evolutionary shift will be different for countries that are divided between fourth and third dimensional areas and countries that are entirely in third dimension. Most countries that are divided will have prepared national leaders. These national leaders will reach out to other national leaders in countries that are divided. Countries that are entirely in third dimension will have unprepared leaders.

Countries Divided Between Third and Fourth Dimensional Areas

People who remain in third dimensional form after the evolutionary shift will be in economic chaos. Many industries will have decreased funds. Money located in fourth dimensional areas will not be available. Thousands of employees will die in earthquakes or transportation accidents during the evolutionary shift and millions of employees will vanish when they evolve to a fourth dimensional form. Economic chaos will be augmented by a decrease in basic necessities such as fuel for transportation, electricity, gas, food and clothing.

Prepared national leaders in countries divided between fourth and third dimensional areas will be ready to address this economic chaos. In addition, they will focus on survival goals. Survival goals will focus on energy distribution, food distribution, young adult child care, economic stability and physical protection.

Although fossil fuels will still be available in third dimensional areas, the transportation of petroleum from the middle east to other areas will stop. National leaders will depend on local oil reserves for electrical power and gasoline. Business owners will work with national leaders to transport needed gas and oil throughout the third dimensional areas.

Similarly, national leaders will focus on food distribution. Only thirty percent of the adult population will remain in third dimensional form. Therefore, there will be fewer people to grow and produce food products and fewer truck drivers to deliver the food. Business owners will work with national leaders to produce and transport food. Local communities will develop community gardens. Small farms producing vegetables and meat products will be supported.

Many of the third dimensional young adults will not have parental supervision. Prepared individuals will help local communities develop foster care and educational experiences for these young adults. In addition, national leaders will develop group homes that will provide education for these young adults.

National leaders will develop a partnership with business leaders and community leaders to help stabilize the economy. Business leaders and community leaders will identify skills and experiences needed and help new employees relocate. Many jobs will be available.

Local community leaders will become responsible for local community protection. People functioning at a lower base frequency level of fear, control and physical violence will be managed by local law enforcement. Private citizens will develop a partnership with law enforcement to provide support.

Third Dimensional Nations

Nations that are completely in third dimension will have unprepared leaders. People in these countries will begin the first year after the evolutionary shift in shock, fear and despair.

Third dimensional individuals will still have the mental construct of competition. People with more money will have more access to basic necessities. Rich people will become frightened of the poor and begin to isolate themselves for economic protection. Homeless people will initially build cardboard societies with the hope that local governments will provide relief. When relief does not come, many homeless will seek shelter in homes and buildings that have been vacated because the previous owners have died or evolved to fourth dimensional form. As the polarization between the rich and poor increases during the first year, poor people will become desperate. Rioting will begin and major cities will be destroyed.

In these nations, social chaos will develop. Homeless people will organize into local groups for protection. Local police forces will not have enough manpower or financial resources to manage the increase in violence and crime. The rich will become more and more frightened. This fear will enhance the polarization between those who have money and those who do not. The rich will isolate themselves more and begin to live behind guarded walls.

Social status will become more polarized. Those with money will have more access to police protection, food, clothing and basic services, such as food, water and electricity. In addition, medical services will be provided to those with money. Health insurance companies will no longer exist, and local governments will not have the resources to support medical services for the poor.

Out of the chaos will come a new world leader for the third dimensional nations. Five months after the vanishings, the antichrist will come to power offering peace and stability. The antichrist will provide a false explanation for the vanishings. People in the third dimensional nations will believe this fabrication and will see the antichrist as a man of peace. The antichrist will encourage all third dimensional nations to unite under his leadership in order to bring stability.

By the end of the first year after the evolutionary shift, all third dimensional nations will unite under the leadership of the antichrist. The antichrist will control the banking industry and all global communication within third dimensional nations.

Third Dimensional Areas - Year Two

The primary goal for souls that are still in third dimensional form is to evolve to fourth dimensional form. Some of the people in third dimensional form have souls that chose to stay in third dimensional form to help others evolve. Other people in third dimensional form are not ready to evolve from the need to control others and the need for physical violence to love, compassion and peace.

Parents who lost children during the evolutionary shift can have hope. These children are still alive and well in fourth dimensional form.

Fourth dimensional people are taking care of these children until the parents evolve.

Migration

At the beginning of the second year following the evolutionary shift, the Creator will send messengers, healers and protectors into the third dimensional areas within the United States of America. This region will be first because the United States of America will have the most resistance to the antichrist and the idea of a global ruler.

The messengers will tell people about Earth's change in rotation, Earth's increased electrical pulse frequency and the truth about the vanishings. In addition, these messengers will teach people about the soul and how the soul uses Earth as a school to learn lessons. People in third dimension will learn about the ongoing battle between people who follow the antichrist and people who believe in the Creator. These messengers will remind people that their primary goal is love and compassion.

The healers will instruct people on how to evolve to fourth dimensional form. Thousands of people will believe these messengers and work with these healers. These people will learn how to heal their karmic fears related to physical violence.

Once people have healed their karmic fears and they no longer need to control others with physical violence, they will evolve from third dimensional form to fourth dimensional form. People who are still in third dimensional form will not be able to see the people who have evolved and a second vanishing will begin. These vanishings will frighten the people who chose not to believe the messengers sent by the Creator.

The protectors will transport people who evolve to fourth dimensional form to a fourth dimensional area. Parents and children who were separated during the evolutionary shift will be reunited.

Food, shelter and medical care will be provided. Jobs and homes within the initial fourth dimensional areas will be offered.

After three months, the messengers, healers and protectors will leave the United States of America and go to Canada, Japan, Australia and New Zealand. At the same time, one third of the third dimensional area in the United States of America will change to fourth dimensional form (Fig 4).

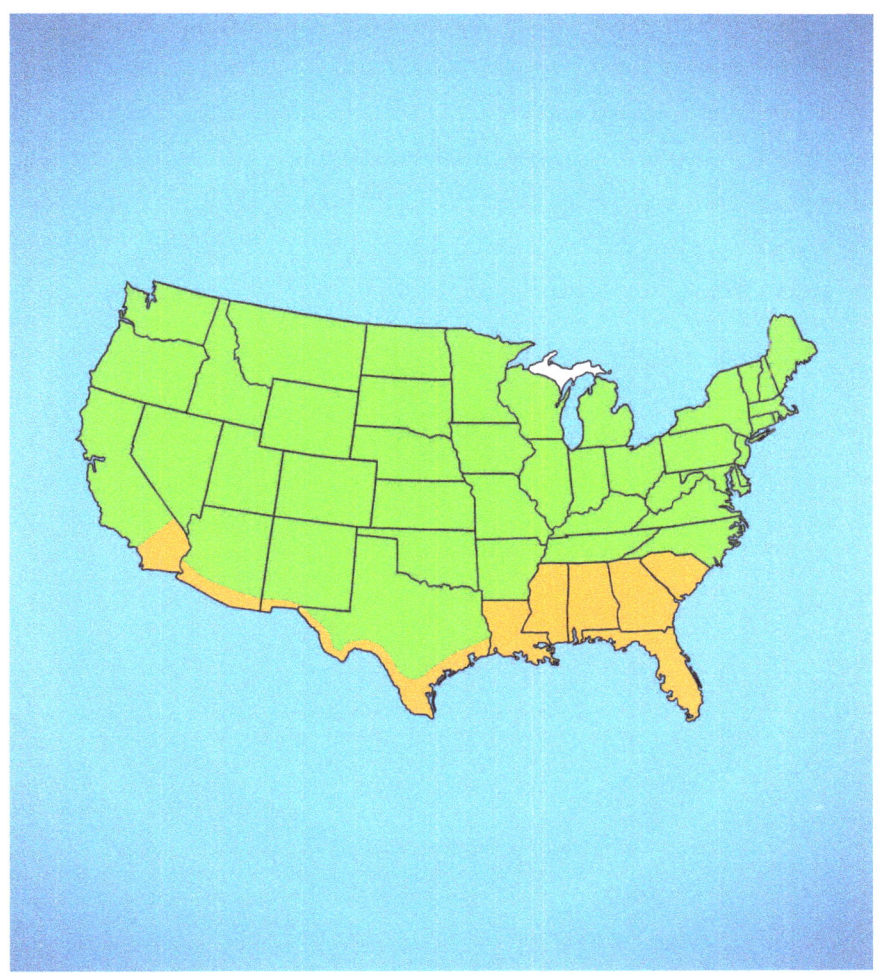

Fig 4
"Post Shift Year Two"
Green = 4th dimensional areas
Orange = 3rd dimensional areas

At the beginning of the seventh month of the second year following the evolutionary shift, the messengers, healers and protectors will leave Canada, Japan, Australia and New Zealand and go to Europe, India, Indonesia, Russia and Peru. At the same time, one half of the third dimensional areas in Canada and Australia will evolve to fourth dimensional form. Similarly, all of Japan and New Zealand will evolve to fourth dimensional form.

At the beginning of the tenth month of the second year following the evolutionary shift, the messengers, healers and protectors will leave Europe, India, Indonesia, Russia and Peru. Messengers will be sent to countries that are totally in third dimension. At the same time, one third of the third dimensional areas in Europe and Russia will evolve to fourth dimensional form. Similarly, one half of India and all of Indonesia and Peru will evolve to fourth dimensional form (Fig 5).

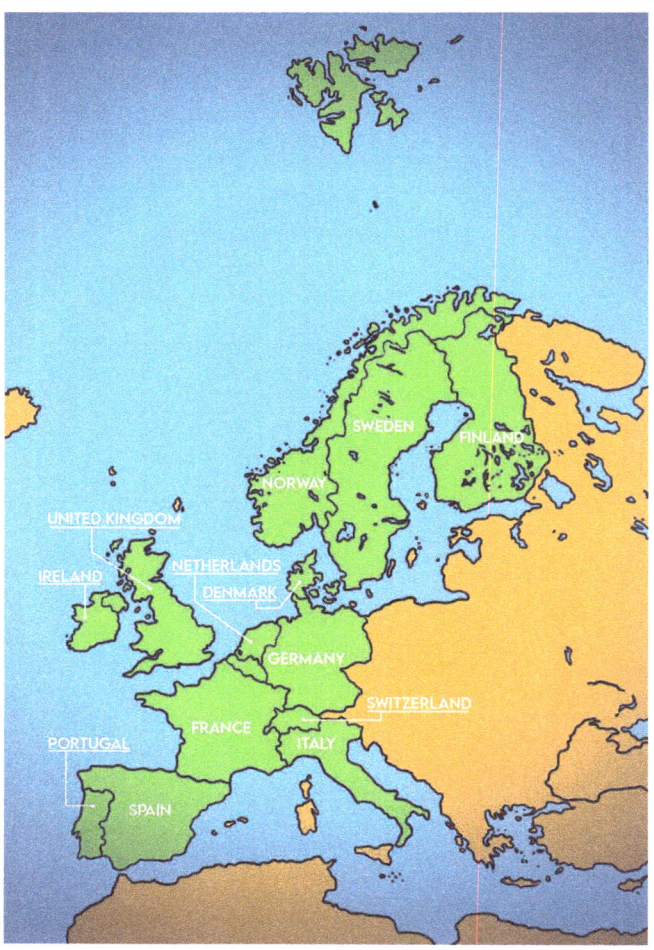

Fig 5
"Post Shift Year Two"
Green = 4th dimensional areas
Orange = 3rd dimensional areas

Antichrist

The antichrist will turn his attention to the fourth dimensional areas during the second year after the evolutionary shift. Third dimensional beings will not be able to see fourth dimensional beings. Therefore, a ground assault will not be effective. If unchecked, the antichrist will attack the fourth dimensional areas from the air.

Resistance toward the antichrist will begin the second year after the evolutionary shift. Primary resistance will develop in nations that are divided between fourth and third dimensional areas. The people in these geographically divided areas will be use to national independence and will resist the concept of global unity under the antichrist. Unfortunately, by the time resistance begins, the antichrist will have control of all nuclear weapons, all financial institutions and all news media. All national governments within nations that are fully third dimensional will be aligned with the antichrist. Resistance to the antichrist will be covert.

Initial resistance to the antichrist will begin with the people believing in Christianity. Christians will not believe the rational for the vanishings offered by the antichrist. Instead, Christians will believe that the vanishings are related to the rapture (Christ coming and taking his chosen to heaven). They will believe that the rapture correlates with the First Seal in the Book of Revelation, and the antichrist represents the Second Seal in the Book of Revelation.

The antichrist will not be able to relieve third dimensional famine related to a food shortage throughout third dimensional areas.

Thousands of people will starve and die. Christians will relate this famine to the Third Seal in the Book of Revelation.

The polarization between the rich and poor will widen during the second year. People will organize into small groups for protection. Those with financial resources will hire bodyguards for protection and live and work behind guarded walls. The poor will organize into groups with weapons for protection. Physical violence will increase with the police unable to protect the poor. The Christians will correlate the increase in deaths related to physical violence with the Fourth Seal of the Book of Revelation.

To counter the resistance by the Christians, the antichrist will propose a single global religion designed to unite all religious groups. This new global religion will profess to accept all faiths. God will be one aspect of this new religion. Belief in God, however, will not be required.

People will be encouraged to accept that "nature" is equal to "God" in all things.

Development of this single global religion will increase the resistance to the antichrist. People of the Jewish and Islamic faiths will join the Christians in the underground resistance.

An underground communication system will develop that will include all people who continue to believe in God. Many religious leaders who speak out against the single global religion will be enemies of the antichrist. Some of these leaders will be killed by the antichrist. Other religious leaders will become refugees and hide. The overall result will be an increase in love and compassion within the people involved in the resistance.

In response to the single global religion, the Creator will send the two witnesses prophesied in the Book of Revelation. These two witnesses will appear wearing sackcloth in Jerusalem. They will praise God and preach that the people should return to God. In addition, they will praise the message of love and compassion provided by Jesus Christ. They will preach against the antichrist. To prove that they are sent by God, they will announce that no rain will fall on Israel until the time of their preaching is over.

The antichrist will be unable to harm these two witnesses during the second year after the evolutionary shift because they will be protected by the Creator. Anyone attempting to harm the witnesses will be devoured by fire coming out of the mouths of the witnesses.

The appearance of the two witnesses will strengthen the underground resistance to the antichrist. Many people will secretly worship God and increase their love and compassion as taught by Jesus Christ.

Toward the end of the second year following the evolutionary shift, a third dimensional global war will break out. The underground resistance will attempt to overthrow the antichrist. Christians will relate this war to the Fifth Seal in the Book of Revelation.

Just before the underground resistance attempts to overthrow the antichrist, fourth dimensional healers and protectors will be sent into all third dimensional areas within nations that are divided between third and fourth dimension (United States, Canada, Europe, Australia, India and Russia). These healers will change the form of all children born during the first two years following the evolutionary shift to fourth dimensional form. Children in these areas will disappear. The protectors will transport these children to a fourth dimensional area.

The souls coming to Earth as children in third dimensional areas, within nations that are divided between third and fourth dimensional areas, are coming to bring more love and compassion to Earth. These children are not coming with the need to suffer. At the time these children begin to vanish, the antichrist will be rising to power.

Thousands of people will be starving, and physical violence will be increasing. All children in these areas will vanish before the third dimensional global war begins.

By the time the underground resistance is ready to attack, the antichrist will control all nuclear weapons. The antichrist will have a global "peace keeping" force which will have more military power than those in the resistance. The antichrist will control all news media. Only the news favorable to the antichrist will be reported. The members of the resistance will be out numbered, have less military power and will not be supported by the news media. This third dimensional global war will be very destructive and very short.

The third dimensional global war will be over by the end of the second year after the evolutionary shift. Following the war, the antichrist will be in control of the third dimensional areas. Nations wanting to rebuild their infrastructure will be required to pledge their allegiance to the antichrist and the third dimensional global community. Global "peace keeping" forces will have authority over local police forces and people will be required to believe what the antichrist wants them to believe.

Fourth Dimensional Areas - Year Two

The primary focus in the fourth dimensional areas during the first year after the evolutionary shift will be the stabilization of local communities. At the beginning of the second year after the evolutionary shift, local communities will be stabilized. Basic community services involving communication, transportation, energy for heating, cooling, cooking and waste disposal will be provided in all fourth dimensional areas. People will be rebuilding the infrastructure, buildings and homes that were damaged in the earthquakes during the evolutionary shift. Basic necessities, including food, clothing, medical services and jobs, will be provided for everyone.

National Governments

People in the fourth dimensional areas will begin to reassess the function of their national governments at the end of the first year after the evolutionary shift. At the beginning of the second year after the evolutionary shift, people in every nation in the fourth dimensional areas will choose to reorganize their national governments. People who are interested in national leadership will be selected to study the needs for each nation.

The focus of national governments in the fourth dimensional areas will be to provide services for the citizens within their own nation. National services involving health care, transportation and communication will be organized. National governments will also focus on facilitating local businesses, job training and employment opportunities.

Fourth dimensional national leaders will focus on helping people who begin migrating from third dimensional areas to fourth dimensional areas. During the entire second year, people in third dimensional areas will be evolving to fourth dimensional form. These people will migrate to fourth dimensional areas to survive. Children who migrate to fourth dimensional areas during the first nine months of the second year will migrate with their families.

The migration of people from third dimensional areas to fourth dimensional areas during the second year after the evolutionary shift will present a challenge to the people living in the fourth dimensional areas. People migrating into the fourth dimensional areas will initially be housed in refugee camps. Food, clothing and medical care will be provided by national and regional governments, business leaders and local communities. Medical care will include both physical and energy healing. Work related skills will be assessed and people will be matched with potential employers. When ready, some of these people will be relocated close to their new employment and homes will be provided.

Children who vanish from third dimensional areas just before the third dimensional global war will be rescued and migrate to fourth dimensional areas without their parents. These children will need immediate foster care. The mental construct of people living in fourth dimensional areas will be that all children must live with a family.

Many people will volunteer to be foster parents. National governments will store the DNA of these foster children to allow them to be reunited with their parents, when their parents evolve to fourth dimensional form.

Business Leaders

While leaders in national governments are focusing on providing services for their citizens, business leaders will begin to focus on developing global trade. Without national governments to restrict trade between nations, global trade within the fourth dimensional areas will flourish. The mental construct for all people in fourth dimensional areas will be one of cooperation and partnership.

Everyone will benefit from global trade.

In addition to establishing global trade markets within the fourth dimensional areas, businesses will develop global communications. Massive advances in communication and transportation technologies will develop in fourth dimensional areas during the second year after the evolutionary shift. Technological advances will develop in areas of food production and distribution.

Business and national leaders will work together to form new communities and businesses in newly formed fourth dimensional areas. Three months into the second year after the evolutionary shift, some third dimensional areas will evolve to fourth dimensional form. People who originally lived in these areas may wish to move back.

By the end of the second year after the evolutionary shift, national leaders will be ready to assist in the development of a new global economy. The precedents of free trade, global cooperation and partnership among nations will already be established by business leaders.

Education

Business leaders will set the precedent for child-care and education of children and young adults during the second year after the evolutionary shift. At the beginning of the second year, all major businesses will begin to provide child-care for the children of their employees. Teaching children in an atmosphere of cooperation and partnership will become a priority. Business leaders who do not have the financial resources to provide child-care will join with other business leaders in a cooperative effort, and child-care will become a benefit for everyone.

Children in fourth dimensional areas will be more evolved and more balanced than children have been in the past. These children will bring in more love and compassion energy. These children will learn to communicate at a much earlier age. Intellectually and emotionally they will develop faster. All children will have an interest in theater arts, music, visual arts and sports. People who are responsible for child-care will prepare a curriculum that meets the needs of these children. Employers will organize the work hours of their employees so that they can volunteer their time coaching organized sports activities or teaching music, visual arts, theater and technical information.

At the beginning of the sixth month during the second year after the evolutionary shift, business leaders will become involved with the curriculum of elementary and secondary schools. Although public schools will be reestablished during the first year after the evolutionary shift, decreased funding and a lack of teachers will require that school curriculums focus on technical content. Music, theater, visual arts and sports activities will not be offered.

Business leaders will take the new approach to child-care and introduce a new teaching philosophy for elementary and secondary schools. Community and regional leaders will develop a partnership with business leaders to implement this new teaching philosophy. An atmosphere of cooperation and partnership between the teachers and students will develop. Businesses will help provide financial and personnel resources to public schools. Music, visual arts and theater arts will be introduced into both elementary and secondary education. In addition, organized sports will return to elementary and secondary education.

Since the mental construct for people in fourth dimensional areas will be one of nonviolence, physical violence during sports activities will no longer exist. Sports where skill is the primary focus will return to the public schools (basketball, soccer, wrestling, track, tennis and golf). The age of American football will be over.

At the same time business leaders are focusing on developing curriculums for child-care, university and college leaders will begin to focus on reorganizing university and college degree programs.

Colleges and universities will be closed during the first year following the evolutionary shift. People will be focused on economic stabilization. All higher education will be put on hold.

The focus on higher education will return to the fourth dimensional areas at the beginning of the second year following the evolutionary shift. University and college leaders will begin meeting to discuss degree programs. More emphasis will be placed on developing learning strategies that encourage cooperation and a partnership between professors and students. Technical programs will be restructured to emphasize both technical information and employee management. Business management programs will focus on developing a partnership among employers, supervisors and employees.

Many college and university degree programs will be reorganized. For example, medical school curriculums will change their focus from the treatment of disease to the prevention of disease. Doctors in fourth dimensional areas will learn about the energy system as well as the physical systems of the body. Techniques that are considered alternative medical approaches in third dimensional areas will become part of fourth dimensional medical curriculums. Doctors will learn how to prevent disease by healing the energy system. Similar curriculum changes will be made in veterinary schools. Veterinarians will become experts at the prevention of disease by healing the energy systems of animals.

By the end of the second year following the evolutionary shift, colleges and universities will be ready to open with the new curriculums in place. While people in third dimensional areas are participating in a third dimensional global war, people in fourth dimensional areas will be focused on improving the education of children and young adults.

Third Dimensional Areas – Year Three

At the beginning of the third year after the evolutionary shift, people in third dimensional form will be divided into two groups. One group of people will not be ready to give up their need to control and their need for physical violence. The second group will form a resistance to fight the antichrist.

To help the resistance, the Creator will send messengers, healers and protectors into third dimensional areas within the United States, Central America, Canada and Australia. In addition, messengers, healers and protectors will be sent to Thailand, Malaysia, Philippines, South Korea, Costa Rica, Panama, French Guiana, Suriname, Paraguay, Uruguay, Guyana and Ecuador.

People who believe in God will be more willing to listen to the messengers this time. The third dimensional global war between the resistance fighting the antichrist and the followers of the antichrist will be over. Basic necessities (food, water, electricity, clothing and fuel for transportation) will be in short supply. Parents who lost their children months before will be seeking answers related to the vanishings. Thousands of Christians, as well as members of the Jewish and Islamic faiths, will heal their karmic fears related to physical violence. These people will evolve to fourth dimensional form.

Protectors will transport these people to a fourth dimensional area.

The antichrist will counter the message sent by the Creator and proclaim that the vanishings are a man-made phenomenon. Since children in the areas where the people are the most supportive to the antichrist will not be vanishing, the antichrist will proclaim that only people who do not support him have the potential of losing their children. Thousands of people will believe the antichrist and refuse to believe the messengers sent by the Creator.

The primary goal of the antichrist at the beginning of the third year after the evolutionary shift will be the rebuilding of the third dimensional areas. Under the umbrella of peace and global unity, the antichrist will begin to rebuild cities that were destroyed in the third dimensional global war. Nations that voluntarily provide significant resources to the antichrist will receive help with the rebuilding of their infrastructure (roads, highways, airports). Many of the nations that are divided between third and fourth dimensional areas will refuse to provide significant resources to the antichrist and will be considered enemies.

The vanishings within the United States, Canada, Australia, Central America, South America and Asia will end just before a great earthquake occurs in the third dimensional areas during the third month of the third year after the evolutionary shift. Before the earthquake begins, the sun will become black and the moon will become as red as blood. Meteors will shower the third dimensional areas just after the earthquake begins. Thousands of people will die and many cities will be destroyed.

After the earthquake, the Creator will change all of the third dimensional areas within the United States, Central America, Canada and Australia to fourth dimensional form. Similarly, Thailand, Malaysia, Philippines, South Korea, Costa Rica, Panama, French Guiana, Suriname, Paraguay, Uruguay, Guyana and Ecuador will be changed to fourth dimensional form (Fig 6).

In addition, after the earthquake, God will send messengers, healers and protectors into the remaining third dimensional areas in Western Europe, India and Russia. In addition, messengers, healers and protectors will be sent to Nepal, Tibet, Eastern Europe and Israel.

Fig 6
"Post Shift Year Three"
Green = 4th dimensional areas
Orange = 3rd dimensional areas

Thousands of people in these areas will heal their karmic fears related to physical violence. These people will evolve to fourth dimensional form. Protectors will transport these people to a fourth dimensional area.

Christians will believe that the earthquake represents the Sixth Seal of the Book of Revelation. Their underground message will profess that the destructions came from the wrath of God toward followers of the antichrist and the single global religion.

In response to the increased love and compassion among the people in the underground resistance to the antichrist, the Creator will place a cross on the foreheads of all members of the resistance to the antichrist. The followers of the antichrist will not be able to see this mark of the Creator. Christians will believe that this cross represents the beginning of the Seventh Seal of the Book of Revelation. The primary purpose of this cross will be to allow members of the resistance to recognize each other. This easy recognition will strengthen the underground resistance to the antichrist.

During the fifth month of the third year after the evolutionary shift, a hailstorm will cover the entire third dimensional areas. Some hail will become fireballs that will set trees and grass on fire. One third of all trees in the third dimensional areas will be destroyed.

During the sixth month of the third year after the evolutionary shift, a comet will strike Earth and create tidal waves in third dimensional areas. Thousands of people in third dimensional areas will die as a result of the destruction along the coastal areas.

Just before the comet strikes Earth, the vanishings in Western Europe, India, Russia, Nepal, Tibet, Eastern Europe and Israel will end. After the comet strikes Earth, the Creator will change all of the remaining third dimensional areas in Western Europe, India, Russia, Nepal and Tibet to fourth dimensional form. Similarly, one half of Eastern Europe will change to fourth dimensional form. All of Israel will stay in third dimension.

Israel will become a primary battleground for the battle between those who follow the antichrist and those members of the Jewish faith who continue to believe in God. The two witnesses will continue to preach against the antichrist. Since these witnesses will also preach the message of Jesus Christ, many members of the Jewish faith will reject the witnesses.

At the beginning of the seventh month during the third year after the evolutionary shift, the Creator will send messengers, healers and protectors into the remaining third dimensional areas in South America. Vanishings in these areas will last until the ninth month.

Just after vanishings begin in South America, a meteor headed for Earth will split into a billion pieces before entering Earth's atmosphere. These meteor fragments will land in rivers, lakes and springs in third dimensional areas and poison the water supply.

Thousands of people in third dimensional areas will die after drinking the poisoned water.

During the eighth month of the third year after the evolutionary shift, the energy sent by the sun will decrease by 33 percent. Since the light from the moon is dependent on the sun, the decrease in sun energy will result in a 33 percent decrease in light energy from the moon.

There will also be a 33 percent decrease in light energy from the stars. The end result will be a 33 percent increase in darkness throughout third and fourth dimensional areas.

The 33 percent decrease in sun energy will create a sudden drop in temperature throughout third and fourth dimensional areas. Winter conditions will develop regardless of the season of the year. These extreme winter conditions will last for two weeks. After a two-week period, the sun and star light energy will return to normal.

The third year after the evolutionary shift will end with the most dramatic sign from the Creator. Locusts will cover the third dimensional areas. Unlike regular locusts, these locusts will have poisonous stingers on their tails.

Just before the locusts cover third dimensional areas, the vanishings in South America will end. The Creator will change all of remaining third dimensional areas in South America to fourth dimensional form.

The locusts will not devour foliage like normal locusts. Instead, they will attack all people who do not have the sealed cross on their foreheads.

People who are stung will not die, although they will certainly pray for death. The sting of the locusts will create severe pain. These locusts will cover third dimensional areas, stinging all people over the age of 18 who do not have the sealed cross for a five- month period of time. No adult without a sealed cross will escape.

Just after the locusts begin to inflict pain and suffering on the people who live in third dimensional areas, a third vanishing of children will begin. Fourth dimensional healers and protectors will go into third dimensional areas in Eastern Europe and Israel. Children in these areas will not need to suffer. The healers will help these children evolve to fourth dimensional form and the protectors will transport these children to a fourth dimensional area.

Fourth Dimensional Areas – Year Three

At the beginning of the third year after the evolutionary shift, people in fourth dimensional areas will reopen colleges and universities.

Curriculums will offer technical, business, teaching and medical programs. There will be a strong emphasis on music, dance, theater and visual arts programs. Musical concerts, dance concerts and theater productions will return at the university level. These concerts and productions will be well attended.

University sports programs will be very popular. All sports programs that focus on skill will return (basketball, baseball, soccer, track, tennis and golf). These sports programs will be designed to allow more students to participate. Thousands of spectators will attend these sports events.

Technological advances will continue. Fourth dimensional communications will become faster and transportation will become more efficient. New technology will allow work environments to become more efficient. Workers in fourth dimensional areas will be able to accomplish more in thirty hours than they were able to accomplish in forty hours before the evolutionary shift.

Employers will reward increased productivity by decreasing the full-time work-week to thirty hours. Employees will receive the same salary and benefits they received for working forty hours. Paid time off will increase. As people learn how to heal their energy systems, employee illness will decrease. Therefore, the increase in paid time off will be spent on vacations.

People in the fourth dimensional areas will have increased leisure time. More emphasis will be placed on family time and most people will volunteer some of their leisure time to working with children.

Secondary and university concerts and sports events will be well attended. In addition, sports activities for adults will be organized and well attended. Vacation time will be spent enjoying and exploring the fourth dimensional areas. The mental construct for people in the fourth dimensional areas will include appreciation for Earth.

The dramatic events happening in the third dimensional areas will not affect the fourth dimensional areas. During the third month of the third year after the evolutionary shift, people in the fourth dimensional areas will see the sun become black and the moon become as red as blood. But, there will not be earthquakes in the fourth dimensional areas. People in the fourth dimensional areas will see the meteor showers coming to Earth, but these meteors will not land in the fourth dimensional areas. People in the fourth dimensional areas will not even be aware of the hailstorm that strikes the third dimensional areas in the fifth month of the third year.

People in the fourth dimensional areas will see the comet coming to Earth during the sixth month of the third year, but tidal waves and flooding will not occur in the fourth dimensional areas. The effect of the comet on the fourth dimensional areas will be an increase in rain. People in the fourth dimensional areas will not even be aware of the meteor fragments that poison the water supply in the third dimensional areas.

The one event that will affect the fourth dimensional areas will be the extreme winter conditions that will occur when the sun energy decreases 33 percent. Unlike the people in third dimensional areas, people in the fourth dimensional areas will be prepared for the sudden drop in temperature. New energy technologies developed by people in fourth dimensional form will allow everyone in fourth dimensional areas to be warm and safe.

The locusts that plague the third dimensional areas will not plague the fourth dimensional areas. These locusts will not enter the fourth dimensional areas.

The migration of people from the third dimensional areas during the third year will continue to present a challenge to the people in the fourth dimensional areas. An even bigger challenge will be the resettlement of the new fourth dimensional areas.

By the end of the third year, the Creator will have changed large segments of land that stayed in third dimensional form immediately after the evolutionary shift to fourth dimensional form. People in third dimensional form still living in these new fourth dimensional areas will migrate to a third dimensional areas to survive. This migration will leave large amounts of vacant land within the fourth dimensional nations. In addition, many nations that were originally all third dimensional form will be divided between third and fourth dimensional areas.

National governments in fourth dimensional areas will have the challenge of coordinating a repopulation of the new fourth dimensional areas. Government leaders will come together to help the new divided nations. Business leaders will develop a partnership with national leaders to help develop new businesses in the new fourth dimensional areas. People will be encouraged to move to the new fourth dimensional areas to find work and homes.

Third Dimensional Areas - Year Four

At the beginning of the fourth year after the evolutionary shift, the Creator will send messengers, healers and protectors into Israel, Mongolia, China, North Korea, Vietnam, Cambodia, Laos, Hong Kong, Singapore and Taiwan. Quan Yin will return to the Asian countries to support the message of love and compassion, explain about the vanishings and life within fourth dimensional areas. She will teach thousands of people how to clear their karmic energies related to control and physical violence. These people will evolve to fourth dimensional form and protectors will transport them to fourth dimensional areas.

In contrast, most people living in Israel will have difficulty believing that there are people on Earth living in fourth dimensional form. The Israelis people will believe in the love and compassion message professed by the two witnesses and will have the sealed cross on their foreheads. They will continue to lead the resistance against the antichrist.

The locusts will continue to plague people in third dimensional areas at the beginning of the fourth year following the evolutionary shift. Millions of people afflicted by the locusts will curse God and align themselves with the antichrist.

In contrast, people not afflicted by the locusts will understand that they are spared because they are in the resistance against the antichrist and they are focused on love and compassion.

Communication among the people in the resistance will improve. These people will develop an underground market for goods and services.

After three months, the Creator will change Mongolia, Hong Kong, Singapore, Taiwan and North Korea to fourth dimensional form.

Similarly, one half of Vietnam, Cambodia and Laos will change to fourth dimensional form. One third of China will change to fourth dimensional form. Israel will remain in third dimensional form.

At the beginning of the fourth month during the fourth year after the evolutionary shift, the Creator will send messengers, healers and protectors into the third dimensional areas in Eastern Europe. The majority of people in these areas will already have the sealed cross on their foreheads. These people will be ready to receive the message about the vanishings and life within the fourth dimensional areas.

During the next three months, most people in these areas will evolve to fourth dimensional form and protectors will transport them to a fourth dimensional area. After three months, one half of the third dimensional areas in Eastern Europe will change to fourth dimensional form.

Fig 7
"Post Shift Year Four"
Green = 4th dimensional areas
Orange = 3rd dimensional areas

The two witnesses sent by the Creator to teach the message of love and compassion will be assassinated during the sixth month of the fourth year following the evolutionary shift. People will be afraid to touch these witnesses and their bodies will lie in the street for three days while thousands of people celebrate the death of the two witnesses. The antichrist will encourage the celebration and declare a victory. People who choose not to follow the antichrist will understand that the time for the witnesses was over and that the Creator's protection was removed.

Three days after the witnesses are assassinated, they will rise in body and again stand before the people in Jerusalem. People who are celebrating will become extremely frightened as an earthquake engulfs Jerusalem killing thousands. Following the earthquake, the bodies of the two witnesses will disappear.

After the resurrection and disappearance of the two witnesses, thousands of people will increase their faith in God and move away from the single global religion. Members of the Christian, Jewish and Islamic faiths will combine to form a stronger resistance to the antichrist.

One month after the two witnesses are assassinated, the antichrist will be assassinated. His body will lie in a casket for three days. After three days, Lucifer will enter the body of the antichrist and the body will be resurrected. The soul of the antichrist will not be resurrected. Instead, the physical body will have a new soul attached.

During the next three months, Lucifer will profess that he is equal to God. By the end of the tenth month during the fourth year following the evolutionary shift, Lucifer will be in control of the single global religion. The single global religion will worship the body of the antichrist.

Just after Lucifer declares that he is equal to God, the Creator will send messengers, healers and protectors back into China. These messengers will encourage people to believe in Buddha's message of love and compassion and teach about the vanishings and life in fourth dimensional areas. In addition, these messengers will profess that Lucifer is not equal to God. Over the next three months, thousands of people in China will evolve to fourth dimensional form. Protectors will transport these people to a fourth dimensional area. After three months, the Creator will change one half of the remaining third dimensional area in China to fourth dimensional form.

By the end of the fourth year following the evolutionary shift, Lucifer will demand that all people in the third dimensional areas join the single global religion and worship the antichrist. To prove their loyalty to Lucifer, people will be required to wear a tattoo on their hand or forehead. This tattoo will be the mark for the single global religion.

People who wear the mark will be allowed to purchase food, clothing and other basic necessities such as electricity, fuel for transportation and telephone service. People who refuse to wear the mark will not be allowed to purchase items within the global community.

The mark will force people who still believe in God to go into hiding. Survival will be based on the black market developed by the resistance to the antichrist.

Children that still live in third dimensional areas in countries that partially evolved to fourth dimensional form did not come to Earth to suffer under the leadership of Lucifer. Therefore, before Lucifer demands that all people join the single global religion, worship the antichrist and wear a tattoo proving their loyalty, the Creator will send healers and protectors into all third dimensional areas in countries that are divided between fourth and third dimension.

Healers will help children in these areas evolve to fourth dimensional form and protectors will transport these children to a fourth dimensional area.

Fourth Dimensional Areas – Year Four

There will be a major energy difference between the people in the third dimensional areas and the people in the fourth dimensional areas at the beginning of the fourth year following the evolutionary shift. People in the third dimensional areas will be divided between people who follow the antichrist and people who believe in God. The people who are following the antichrist will be suffering from the locust stings. The people who believe in God will grow stronger in faith and create a strong underground resistance to the antichrist.

Instead of being divided, the people in the fourth dimensional areas will begin to grow closer to each other. A move toward global unity will develop in three major areas: leisure activities, international business and international travel.

At the beginning of the fourth year following the evolutionary shift, people in the fourth dimensional areas will expand their leisure activities. Professional concerts (music and dance), professional theater and professional sports will return. The mental construct of people will be that these performances are more enjoyable when they experience them live with other people. Professional concerts, theaters and sports will be affordable and available to all people in the fourth dimensional areas.

Television in the fourth dimensional areas immediately following the evolutionary shift will consist of news media. Due to the lack of funds and decreased personnel, television programs not related to news media will not exist.

During the first three years following the evolutionary shift, technological advances will combine computer and communication technologies with television technologies. People will begin to use their televisions for computer technology and communication with each other.

During the fourth year following the evolutionary shift, owners of television stations will begin streaming professional concerts, professional theater and professional sports events live on television. People unable to attend these events in person will be able to enjoy them on television. These events will be global. All people in the fourth dimensional areas will be able to enjoy the professional concerts, professional theater and professional sports events in all fourth dimensional areas.

During the fourth year following the evolutionary shift, the mental construct for people in the fourth dimensional areas will change from what is best for the nation to what is best for the global community. Business leaders will focus on international trade and international corporations. International travel will become easier. People will move freely from one nation to another without the need for passports. By the end of the fourth year following the evolutionary shift, national leaders within the fourth dimensional areas will follow the precedent set by business leaders. National leaders will begin to meet on a regular basis to discuss areas of mutual benefit, cooperation and partnership among nations.

People in the fourth dimensional areas will not be affected by the events in the third dimensional areas during the fourth year following the evolutionary shift. The antichrist will be assassinated and Lucifer will be incarnated without people in the fourth dimensional areas noticing. At the time Lucifer is requiring the mark for the single global religion, people of all religions in the fourth dimensional areas will be discussing cooperation and partnership.

The migration of people from the third dimensional areas during the fourth year after the evolutionary shift will no longer present a challenge to the people in the fourth dimensional areas. The process of assimilating new people, adopting new children and resettling new fourth dimensional areas will be done with love, compassion, cooperation and partnership.

Third Dimensional Areas – Year Five

At the beginning of the fifth year following the evolutionary shift, a battle will begin between the people who worship Lucifer and wear the mark and the people who continue to worship God. The people who refuse to wear the mark of Lucifer will be persecuted. Thousands of people who refuse to wear the mark will be killed.

In response to the resistance to Lucifer, the Creator will once again send messengers, healers and protectors into the third dimensional areas in Vietnam, Cambodia, Laos and China. Quan Yin will return to Asia and reaffirm Buddha's message of love and compassion. People who are able to survive the persecutions of Lucifer will begin to move toward this message of love and compassion. Thousands of people will accept the message about the vanishings and life in the fourth dimensional areas. These people will evolve to fourth dimensional form, and protectors will transport them to a fourth dimensional area. After three months, the Creator will change all of China, Vietnam, Cambodia and Laos to fourth dimensional form.

After five months of persecution and murder, the underground resistance to Lucifer will be stronger than ever. All people believing in God will have the cross on their foreheads. Although people who do not wear the mark of Lucifer will continue to hide, their fear of death will decrease.

At the beginning of the fifth month of the fifth year after the evolutionary shift, the Creator will send messengers, healers and protectors into the third dimensional areas in Eastern Europe. The messengers will work with the members of the resistance, explaining the reason for the vanishings and life in fourth dimensional areas. All members of the resistance will evolve to fourth dimensional form and protectors will transport them to a fourth dimensional area. After three months, almost all of Eastern Europe will change to fourth dimensional form.

During the fifth month of the fifth year after the evolutionary shift, a plague will cross the third dimensional areas. This plague will appear to be contagious and will create open sores over the bodies of the people who wear the mark of Lucifer. People who refuse to wear the mark will not be affected. Physicians will not be able to find the cause for the open sores and traditional medicine will be ineffective.

At the beginning of the eighth month of the fifth year after the evolutionary shift, the Creator will send messengers, healers and protectors into Israel, Jordon and Egypt. Again, the messengers will work with the members of the resistance, explaining the reason for the vanishings and life in fourth dimensional areas. All members of the resistance will evolve to fourth dimensional form and protectors will transport them to a fourth dimensional area.

At the same time the latest group of messengers, healers and protectors go to the middle east a drought will begin in the third dimensional areas. Very little rain will fall in the third dimensional areas and the sun energy will increase, creating an increase in temperature in both the third and fourth dimensional areas. The highest temperatures will be within the third dimensional areas, with the temperature increasing to 110 degrees. People in third dimensional areas will have difficulty adjusting to the severe heat.

Thousands of people will die from heat stroke and dehydration.

One month after the severe increase in temperature, Earth's temperature will drop as the sun's energy decreases. The lowest temperatures will be within the third dimensional areas, with the temperature dropping to below zero degrees.

The extreme temperatures will widen the gap between the people who wear the mark of Lucifer and the people who continue to believe in God. People who wear the mark will attribute the extreme temperature changes to a punishment. These people will continue to support Lucifer as he tries to rule the third dimensional areas.

Members of the resistance to Lucifer's rule will increase their love and compassion energy and begin to demonstrate this love and compassion energy toward people who wear the mark of Lucifer. In response to the increased love and compassion energy demonstrated by members of the resistance, the Creator will increase the sun energy and normal temperatures will return to the third dimensional areas.

People who wear the mark of Lucifer will receive conflicting messages after Earth's temperature returns to normal. Lucifer will claim responsibility for increasing the sun energy. The underground resistance will profess that God's love and compassion was responsible for returning Earth's temperature to normal.

People who believe in God will begin to understand that God loves and accepts all people. They will also understand that death does not affect the soul. These people will demonstrate peace and a lack of fear when they are persecuted and executed.

People who wear the mark of Lucifer will begin to notice the sense of peace, lack of fear, love and compassion coming from the enemies of Lucifer. They will notice a direct contrast to the hatred, fear and control embodied in Lucifer. Many people who wear the mark will move toward love and compassion.

A third group of people will develop. Thousands of people who originally received the mark of Lucifer will become part of the resistance and receive the cross on their foreheads. Secretly, this third group of people will help the people who are hiding.

In addition, this third group of people will begin to listen to the messengers teaching about the vanishings and life in the fourth dimensional areas. The members of this third group of people will evolve to fourth dimensional form, and protectors will transport them to a fourth dimensional area.

Toward the end of the fifth year following the evolutionary shift, all of Israel will be changed to fourth dimensional form. One third of Jordon and Egypt will be changed to fourth dimensional form.

Just after the preceding areas change to fourth dimensional form, a great earthquake will cover the third dimensional areas. Major cities in the third dimensional areas will be destroyed and thousands of people will die. The fifth year will end with Lucifer rebuilding again.

Fourth Dimensional Areas – Year Five

There will be a large difference between the quality of life for people in the third dimensional areas and the quality of life for people in the fourth dimensional areas during the fifth year following the evolutionary shift. People in the third dimensional areas will experience illness and death. This will be a dark time for people who continue to follow Lucifer. The followers of Lucifer will be consumed with fear.

In contrast, people in the fourth dimensional areas will be focused on healing their physical bodies by healing their energy systems, decreasing their fear and increasing their love and compassion.

Business leaders will once again take the lead by providing educational workshops and retreats related to healing the energy system of human bodies. Nature essences, healing energy cysts that help create physical disease and pain, and healing emotional pain will be emphasized. In addition, business leaders will support workshops and retreats designed to teach how to improve energy relationships among human beings. People in the fourth dimensional areas will improve their physical and emotional health.

During the fifth year after the evolutionary shift, business leaders will invest in the movie industry. Due to decreased funding and a lack of personnel, the movie industry will not exist immediately after the evolutionary shift. When people in the fourth dimensional areas return to leisure entertainment, they will be more interested in live performances than performances on film. However, the interest in performances on film will return during the fifth year.

Since the mental constructs of people will no longer support physical violence, movies in the fourth dimensional areas will not display physical violence. Villains will be people who perform energy violations by introducing fear and anger into communities or by stealing energy from other people. Heroes will be people who block these energetic violations, help other people physically and provide love and compassion energy.

The other major difference with fourth dimensional movies will be in the way people view movie stars. Actors and actresses will be seen as entertainers trying to bring love and compassion to the community.

These people will be valued the same as other entertainers. The age of worshiping movie stars will be over.

People in the fourth dimensional areas will be unaffected by the plague of open sores during the fifth month of the fifth year. Similarly, the earthquake at the end of the fifth year following the evolutionary shift will not affect fourth dimensional areas.

In contrast, the extreme temperature changes on Earth during the eighth and ninth months of the fifth year following the evolutionary shift will affect fourth dimensional areas. People in the fourth dimensional areas will be prepared. Outdoor activities will be limited. In preparation for the two months, water and food will be stored by national governments and distributed to all people. In addition, electricity for air-conditioning and heat and warm clothing will be provided to all people in the fourth dimensional areas.

EPILOGUE

At the beginning of the sixth year following the evolutionary shift, Earth will stabilize. The following areas will remain in third dimensional form under the rule of Lucifer: Turkiye, Iran, Iraq, Afghanistan, Pakistan, Syria, Yemen, Oman, Lebanon, Jordan, Saudi Arabia and Africa. All other areas on Earth will be in fourth dimensional form. This Earth stabilization will hold for 20-30 years.

"Post Shift Year Five"
Green = 4th dimensional areas
Orange = 3rd dimensional areas"

People in the fourth dimensional areas will thrive. They will strive to increase their love and compassion and improve their life experience on Earth. Everyone will be economically stable. Technological advances, as well as educational advances in medicine and liberal arts will improve the quality of life for the people living in the fourth dimensional areas.

People in the fourth dimensional areas will form a partnership between medical personnel and patients, teachers and students, and employers and employees. Individuals will become responsible for their own health and medical care. Physicians will provide diagnoses and treatment suggestions. Students will become responsible for their own learning. Teachers will become guides. Parents will be more involved with their children's education. Employees will share responsibility for the success of their employers.

In contrast, at the beginning of the sixth year following the evolutionary shift, Lucifer will rule the third dimensional areas. He will rule with fear, control and terror.

People who continue to live in third dimensional areas will be divided into two groups. The first group will consist of people who continue to function at the second chakra level, dominated by fear and control energies. This group will follow Lucifer. The second group will consist of people who function at the fourth chakra level, dominated by love and compassion energies. This second group will form a resistance movement to the reign of Lucifer.

The people on Earth will be able to influence the length of Lucifer's reign in the third dimensional areas. If messengers, healers and protectors from the fourth dimensional areas are willing to continue the battle in the third dimensional areas beyond the first five years after the evolutionary shift, the time for Lucifer's reign will decrease significantly. The message of love and compassion from the fourth dimensional areas will bring hope, peace and strength to the people in the third dimensional areas. As more people move toward the peace associated with love and compassion energy, Lucifer's power will weaken.

Vanishings will continue in the third dimensional areas. People moving toward love and compassion energy will clear their karmic fears related to physical violence. They will accept the message about life in the fourth dimensional areas and evolve to fourth dimensional form. Protectors will transport these people to a fourth dimensional area.

When the number of people evolving toward love and compassion in the third dimensional areas reaches critical mass, Lucifer's reign will end. Over a three-year period, the remaining third dimensional areas will change to fourth dimensional form.

ABOUT THE AUTHOR

 Kathleen believes in a loving Creator who assists all human beings by sending them messages. At the age of 49, the Creator sent Kathleen a messenger. Kathleen met with this messenger for a total of ten hours and then the messenger sent the message in writing. The messenger provided all of the information about the evolutionary shift, the healing tools and how to clear karmic energies.

As a learner centered teacher, Kathleen's goal is to help others learn and prepare for the evolutionary shift. Kathleen understands that human beings learn through repetition. Therefore, she is providing information about the evolutionary shift and how to prepare for the evolutionary shift in her book, Preparing for the Shift. In addition, she is providing information with videos on YouTube. For those of you who choose to prepare, Kathleen will offer conference calls on zoom.

www.ingramcontent.com/pod-product-compliance
Lightning Source LLC
Chambersburg PA
CBHW051216120626
46547CB00013B/1375